GREEN

Container

Gardening

This is a **FLAME TREE** book
First published in 2012

Publisher and Creative Director: Nick Wells
Senior Project Editor: Catherine Taylor
Project Editor and Copy Editor: Caroline West
Art Director: Mike Spender
Layout Design: Dave Jones
Digital Design and Production: Chris Herbert
Picture Research: Caroline West
Proofreader: Dawn Laker
Indexer: Helen Snaith

Special thanks to: Stephen Feather, Laura Bulbeck and Laura Zats

12 14 16 15 13
1 3 5 7 9 10 8 6 4 2

This edition first published 2012 by
FLAME TREE PUBLISHING
Crabtree Hall, Crabtree Lane
Fulham, London SW6 6TY
United Kingdom
www.flametreepublishing.com

Flame Tree Publishing is part of The Foundry Creative Media Co. Ltd

ISBN 978-0-85775-387-8

Many thanks to **Burgon & Ball** (www.burgonandball.com) for supplying the image on page 177.

Images © **Peter Anderson**: 104t, 104b, 105l, 105r, 114b, 115l, 115r, 116l, 116r, 118r.

Courtesy of Wikimedia Commons/Division of Plant Industry Archive, Florida Department of Agriculture and Consumer Services, United States/Bugwood.org (public domain): 247; Zapyon/GNU Free
Documentation License/Creative Commons license Attribution-Noncommercial-Share Alike 3.0 Unported license: 245 & 246.

Courtesy of **Shutterstock.com** and © the following contributors: 1 &120t, 11, 14b, 119t, 119b Elena Elisseeva; 3 & 173b Berislav Kovacevic; 4t & 17, 64b, 86, 87l Dirk Ott; 4b & 39, 45, 68, 188
Richard Griffin; 5t & 63 Maximus Art; 5b & 85 Melanie Kintz; 6t & 125 luminouslens; 6b & 167 KellyNelson; 7t & 187 keith robinson; 7b JEO; 8, 35t, 134, 144r, 239 Ivonne Wierink; 9t David Kay; 9b &
231l, 100r, 142l, 181c, 225 Tamara Kulikova; 10 CLM; 12l, 15, 23bt, 50 Marie C Fields; 12r, 174 Sheri Armstrong; 13 Alistair Cotton; 14t Brenda Carson; 18l snowblurred; 18r mypokcik; 19t SF photo;
19b H. Brauer; 20bl Triff; 20cr HixnHix; 20tl Tereza Dvorak; 21t, 195l Sally Scott; 21b Elena Fernandez Zabelguelskaya; 22t, 49tr, 206, 209 Nic Neish; 22b Kirk Peart Professional Imaging; 23bl Ingrid
Balabanova; 23br Stephanie Frey; 24l Sakala; 24r, 132t Christopher Elwell; 25l Robert Adrian Hillman; 25r Anteromite; 26l M. Cornelius; 26r, 60l, 60r c.byatt-norman; 27 Dmitry Rukhlenko; 28br John
Holst; 28l Kasia; 28tr Sayanski; 29l Sandra van der Steen; 29r Richard Peterson; 30l Stacy Barnett; 30r Loskutnikov; 31t, 181t Lynn Watson; 31b, 59 Jorge Salcedo; 32, 143 Videowokart; 33bl Nneirda;
33br Elena Butinova; 33tl Bochkarev Photography; 34 Dhoxax; 35b Ken Schulze; 36l, 114t, 132b, 136 V. J. Matthew; 36r sarka; 40l Thomas M Perkins; 40r Timothy Large; 41l Simone van den Berg;
41r Steven Belanger; 43 hagit berkovich; 44 Valery Kraynov; 46bl Juriah Mosin; 46br, 243 Mayovskyy Andrew; 46t Norma Cornes; 47l, 49bl, 47l, 51l, 176 Brandon Blinkenberg; 47r Jonathan Lenz; 48
David Hughes; 49br Fabio Alcini; 51r ultimathule; 52l Robert Pernell; 52r Kateryna Larina; 53b wheatley; 53t, 172l GraŞa Victoria; 54b Shannon West; 54t, 147l Svetlana Turilova; 55b Marjanneke de
Jong; 55t Soundsnaps; 56l Olga Utlyakova; 56r, 121 abimages; 57b Alon Brik; 57c dcwcreations; 57t Wayne R; 58b Rie Carroll; 58t Irineos Maliaris; 64t Chrislofoto; 65 DUSAN ZIDAR; 66l, 99tl, 117r,
155 LianeM; 66r Mindy w.m. Chung; 67b, 82b Alena Brozova; 67t grafoto; 69b mates; 69t pixmac; 70l Elaine Davis; 70r Luis César Tejo; 71, 205 Christina Richards; 72l Rosamund Parkinson; 72r
Andrei Rybachuk; 73 Benjamin F. Haith; 74 Kameel4u; 75t Mark Herreid; 75b, 161l Wouter Tolenaars; 76 leungchopan; 77l jeff gynane; 77r Amanda Herron; 79l ricardomiguel.pt; 78 Raw.lik.2; 79r
Santje09; 80 Cheryl A. Meyer; 81bl pixelman; 81br D. Kucharski & K. Kucharska; 81tr FILATOV ALEXEY; 82t Petr Jilek; 87r Evgeny Murtola; 88l AMA; 88r, 137 Lorraine Kourafas; 89br Madlen; 89tl, 92l
grintan; 89tr Teresa Levite; 90l Debbie Vinci; 90r shippee; 91 mythja; 92r photobar; 93 Steven Good; 94 Andresr; 95b Hannamariah; 95t YANGCHAO; 96b Uros Cernigoj; 96t Olena Zaskochenko; 97l
Ruslana Stovner; 97r Evgeny Itsikson; 98bl Melissa Dockstader; 98br JaNell Golden; 98tl SunnyS; 98tr Peder Digre; 99bc Cre8tive Images; 99br carolyn brule; 99tl Matthew Collingwood; 100l Dale
Wagler; 101l, 150t mitzy; 101r katatonia82; 102 Bernd Juergens; 103 yampi; 106l Gina Smith; 106r, 217 Kheng Guan Toh; 108 Danny Munson; 109l Paul Cowan; 109r MarkMirror; 110l Inc; 110r
Krasowit; 111l, 113t, 128 Lijuan Guo; 111r erperlstrom; 112b, 117l Joy Brown; 112r Claudia Carlsen; 113b, 146 Tom Curtis; 118l 1000 Words; 120b Matt Hart; 122b Yuriy Chertok; 122t Feng Yu; 126
LiliGraphie; 127 Patricia Marroquin; 128b Karoline Cullen; 129 Beata Becla; 130, 197, 208r Shebeko; 131, 248 Copit; 132t Christopher Elwell; 133 cycreation; 135t Doug Stacey; 135b Tatiana
Makotra; 138 Kenneth Keifer; 139 Igor Grochev; 140l Vaide Seskauskiene; 140r Scott Latham; 142r Walter Pall; Todd Boland 144l; 145 KAppleyard; 147r Tolchik; 148 martin garnham; 149l Carlos Gi;
149r Philip Eppard; 150b chungking; 151 Brian A Jackson; 152 iwka; 153 Thomas Nord; 154 Drozdowski; 156 Peter Radacsi; 157, 164r Anne Kitzman; 159 Taina Sohlman; 160 matka_Wariatka; 161r
Ivaschenko Roman; 162 Emily Goodwin; 163 Sony Ho; 164l Valerii Kotulskyi; 168 quest; 169 Ruth Harris; 170l Sherri R. Camp; 170r Melinda Fawver; 171l quetton; 171r Eky Studio; 172r Linda Muir;
173t Aleksandar Mijatovic; 175 Maria Sbytova; 178l Wolna; 178r Stocksnapper; 180 Elena Rostunova; 181b Sophie Bengtsson; 182 WH CHOW; 183 Fotomicar; 184l iliuta goean; 184r Bork; 189
Chris Humphries; 191 Mona Makela; 192 withGod; 193 Kzenon; 194 niderlander; 195r Alan Egginton; 196 David Burrows; 198 ndrpggr; 199 Mazzzur; 200l Allison Hays - Allicat Photography; 200r
Teodor Ostojic; 202 6377724229; 203 Irina Fischer; 204 Jim Lopes; 207 DFabri; 208l Steve Lovegrove; 210 Elena Schweitzer; 213 Chubykin Arkady; 214 Alex James Bramwell; 215t Dmytruk Olena;
215b, 222l Jiri Sebesta; 216 Brykaylo Yuriy; 218 simoly; 219 Mary Lane; 221 Imageman; 222r Sofia; 223t Fedor Korolevskiy; 223b Carlos Caetano; 224t mykeyruna; 224b Nancy Tripp; 226 oneo;
227 Ingrid Balabanova; 228 Tina Rencelj; 229 Nikita Tiunov; 230t artis777; 230b loflo69; 231r GeNik; 232 Margit; 233, 236t, 236b PAUL ATKINSON; 234 David Lade; 235 John A. Anderson; 237
ScriptX; 238 Norman Chan; 240 Cathleen A Clapper; 241 Alexandr Shebanov; 242 Elena Blokhina; 244 Claudio Baldini.

GREEN GUIDES
Container
Gardening

ANDREW MIKOLAJSKI

Foreword by ADAM PASCO, Editor, *BBC Gardeners' World Magazine*

FLAME TREE
PUBLISHING

Contents

Enjoying Container Gardening

Whether you are looking for containers for long-term use
or seasonal display, this introduction will guide you through
the many options you'll find in garden centres and DIY stores.
It also gives some hints on customizing containers so that
they'll reflect your individual style and personality. And there's
advice on more unusual containers and how you can choose
suitable plants to grow in them.

Getting Started

You've made your choice of container. Now, you
need to know how to plant it up. What equipment
do you need and where can you source the plants?
Do any plants need a particular type of compost?
Once planted, you can spruce up your containers
with a range of decorative trims to conceal the
compost surface. You can also raise them to
different levels to display them to best advantage.

Care & Maintenance

Plants in containers need the same care as other plants – in some ways, they need more. This chapter explains when to water and feed them to make sure you get the results you want and also what to do when they outgrow their container. Certain plants have stems that benefit from support and many will need pruning to keep them neat and within bounds or dead-heading to prolong flowering. Here's where to find advice on getting plants through the winter and dealing with some common pests and diseases.

Container Designs

Design is an important element of garden-making. A variety of looks can be created with different types of container. Whatever you choose, the way they are placed in an area or grouped together can have quite an impact. Tips on colour theory and scent will help you make choices when you come to combine plants, particularly for seasonal display. There is even a section on making a mini water garden. A style gallery offers some suggestions for plant combinations for various locations.

For help with seasonal planning, advice is given here on plants that look particularly good at certain times of year. There are reminders on what to do when, so you can plan your time properly and get ahead. You'll also find information on containers for year-round interest and tips on how to liven them up with other plants through the year.

Most gardeners have to deal with less than ideal spots from time to time, whether it's a very shady area, a suntrap or a very windy garden. Roof gardens, balconies and terraces pose their own problems, but it's here that containers come into their own, as you can create a garden where there's no soil at all. Plants can even be attached to walls to make maximum use of available space.

Productive Containers 186

You can grow at least some of your own food each year in containers. Many people have a few tomato plants in growing bags for the summer, but there is a whole range of others you can grow – even potatoes. Fruit can be very successful in containers too – not only strawberries, but also figs, blueberries, dwarf apples and peaches. The majority of herbs thrive in containers. You can easily create your own mini potager, even in the smallest space.

Containers Indoors 212

Containers allow you to bring the garden into the house, and it's extraordinary what a wide range of plants will thrive there. You can produce exciting displays with leaves and a few vibrant flowers, while, if it's scent you want, try forcing a few spring hyacinths for flowering in the depths of winter. If space is tight, try a few cacti on a windowsill, which will not grow too fast. Ideally, you'll have room for a few orchids – among the most glamorous of all plants.

Foreword

Creating a garden is one of the most rewarding things you can ever do. There are choices to make, plants to select and care plans to follow, and these are just as important when planning a tiny garden as they are a large one.

Every plant must earn its place, delivering value by being productive or just looking good for as long as possible. For those new to gardening, the choices can be bewildering, which is why a guide like this is so valuable. By providing page after page of advice and inspiration, you will be armed with everything needed to create your perfect container garden.

My own garden is packed with pots, with more swelling their ranks each season. While some plants, like my old agapanthus, have been with me for years and become old friends, other pots are used to create seasonal highlights. Tulips and daffodils are planted to welcome spring, replaced with pelargoniums and petunias for a summer crescendo and then taking the year full circle with a selection of dwarf evergreen shrubs for flower, fruit and foliage that looks good right through winter.

And that's the joy of container gardening. Everything is flexible. Plants in pots are mobile, so as one plant reaches perfection it can be moved to take centre stage while other players are shifted into the wings to provide a supporting role.

Container gardening fires the imagination, providing opportunities to try something new, achievable and affordable. Whether for colour or scent, herbs or fruit, sun or shade, you can create the perfect pot for every season. It's rather like cooking, as with the right ingredients, a good recipe and a little practical flare, you can produce something truly breathtaking!

This essential guide is packed with ideas and information you can trust for choosing and planting pots both inside and outside your home. Follow its advice and you'll be guaranteed a container garden to be proud of.

Happy gardening!

Adam Pasco, Editor, *BBC Gardeners' World Magazine*

Introduction

If gardens are our playground, then plants in containers are our special pets – on which we lavish time and care, and which we keep close to us. Literally so, as many of us have containers near the house, next to the front door or clustered in companionable groups on the patio. Even with no garden at all, it's still possible to have a hanging basket or two attached to the wall or a windowbox as a home for small plants to provide colour and interest. And some plants can lead a very pampered existence in heated living rooms and conservatories.

Unlimited Scope

The joy of container gardening lies in opportunity. Almost any plant can be grown in a pot, so this gives you the option to enjoy all those plants that would not normally thrive in your garden. Maybe your soil wouldn't suit them or it's just too cold in winter. If you live in a frost-prone area, you can still grow citrus and olive trees – and if you have a conservatory, you may even get to enjoy a few fruits.

Some plants actually do better in containers than out of them – it seems that restricting the roots focuses their energies elsewhere. Clivias and agapanthus will flower more freely in pots and figs will bear much better fruits – and more of them.

A Long History

People have been growing plants in containers for as long as they have been gardening. Pots have always been used for rare and precious specimens and for exotics brought – often at great expense – from foreign lands. Crusaders brought plants from the Middle East into western Europe, explorers of the 16th and 17th centuries introduced plants from the New World and Africa, while later centuries saw novelties brought home from the Far East, the Indian subcontinent and Australia. All of these plants were transported in containers, sometimes spending many months in them.

A traditional Islamic courtyard garden would be home to any number of plants in containers and illustrated European manuscripts of the Middle Ages show pots of plants being grown in palaces and monastic gardens. At Versailles, near Paris, Louis XIV had a prized collection of orange trees all grown in their own special tubs that were wheeled outdoors each summer to decorate the garden. Their winter home was a custom-built orangery.

Nowadays, we use containers for all manner of purposes – to bring life to a courtyard, patio or other paved part of a garden, to decorate walls and windowsills, and even to provide food.

A Wealth of Choice

Containers are available in a range of sizes and made from a vast number of materials to suit every need and budget. Large stone or lead containers can be a major investment. The ones you see in the gardens of stately homes may be several centuries old and have probably seen generations of plants (and gardeners) come and go. At the other extreme, plastic containers can

be had for a very modest outlay (and the plants can't tell the difference). Cheapest of all are growing bags in which you simply cut holes for the plants – no container needed.

With just a little imagination you can use household items – customized or not – as containers. Even things that you would ordinarily throw away, such as old paint cans and oil tins, can be put to good use as plant containers. If you can't easily make holes in the base, simply use them as they are and sink a cheap plastic container inside.

Many Uses

Containers can be used throughout the garden. Big containers make excellent focal points and main features in their own right. A large glazed jar or urn strategically placed gives style to any planting scheme.

Use hanging baskets to brighten up a doorway in summer. Windowboxes give colour to windows and can be secured to a balustrade or even hung from a wall or fence. Even a side passage that is predominantly shady can be home to a collection of potted ferns and hostas or become an outdoor retreat for your houseplants in summer. There's hardly a single part of your outdoor space that can't be used to accommodate plants.

Ringing the Changes

Containers allow you to grow different plants each year. You can even move them around every few weeks to change the scenery, especially if they are in lightweight plastic pots. Shrubs and trees can start off in containers, then, when they get too big, you can either plant them out in the garden or pass them on to friends – freeing up the container (and the space it occupied) for other plants.

You can also play around with colour schemes. Try combining different plants in containers and then arrange them in groups until you get the effect you want. You can either replicate this in the garden next year – or do something entirely different. You may fancy having a summer of pastel flowers one year, but then find yourself in the mood for something much more dynamic a year later.

Colour Through the Year

While spring and summer containers can be as bold and brilliant as you like, you can also add colour in the cooler months, particularly if the rest of the garden is bare. Use small berrying shrubs for colour in autumn, and be sure to make full use of winter-flowering heathers, winter pansies, cyclamen and hellebores to brighten up the dark days. Several bulbs flower just after mid-winter and these are all ideal for use in shallow containers and windowboxes.

A well-planned container can be like a big outdoor flower arrangement – with the difference that your plants will last for weeks or even months. Some plants are attractive enough to provide interest throughout the year, either because of their interesting leaves or because of their overall form. Several plants can be clipped to a shape that will make a stylish contribution to the scene whatever the season.

Containers in Garden Design

Containers can play an important part in the design of any garden. Use them to bring seasonal colour to expanses of green, such as a lawn, or raised on a pillar in a shrub border. And, of course, they will liven up a 'dead' space such as a deck or paved area.

Plants in containers can flank a front door to welcome you home, or be on the patio in full view from a sitting-room window to tempt you outdoors.

Carefully chosen, containers can add style to any garden, whether you choose large, imposing tubs or a number of small pots that bring splashes of colour throughout the garden – on patios, by the side of a pool, standing on low walls or along paths.

Plants for Home and Office

Interior spaces come alive – literally – with plants, whether it's just a few cacti and saintpaulias on a windowsill or a larger mixed display using leafy begonias, tall ficus and monstera. With orchids, saintpaulias, sinningias and rainforest cacti, you can also enjoy flowers, often at times when outdoor containers are largely empty. If you're worried about potting compost spilling onto the carpets and furniture, grow the plants hydroponically in water.

Food for Thought

It's surprising the number of edible plants – even fruit trees – that will give good crops in containers. Many people grow tomatoes, but there is a wealth of leafy vegetables that will also thrive in containers. You can even grow potatoes in pots. Herbs are often grown in containers, and just a few pots near the back door or in the kitchen will provide leaves for flavouring all manner of dishes.

Enjoying Container Gardening

Why Use Containers?

All good gardeners, even though they enjoy plunging their hands into good garden soil, love to grow things in containers. Above all, containers give you choice and a greater element of control.

Extending Plant Choice

People who love their plants always want to grow as many as they can – but it's often the case that your soil is just not suitable. Too wet, too stony or too much lime, for instance. Or it may be that you want to use a container to restrict the size of a plant you don't have room for in the garden – so you can grow colonizing grasses and bamboos without the risk that they'll take over.

A Touch of the Tropics

If your garden is in a cold area and you can't easily grow the plants you love to see on your trips abroad – pelargoniums, olive trees, citrus and oleanders – grow them in pots, so you can enjoy them outside during the warmer months, then bring them under cover in winter.

Oleander

Seasonal Display

Containers can be planned to provide a burst of colour in spring – when much of the garden may still be bare – or in summer when many garden plants will already have gone over. It's also possible to make colourful displays for winter interest – you can enjoy pots placed on the patio near a sitting room window, so you don't even need to go outside.

Narcissus

A Moveable Feast

Many people have small gardens, possibly with no room for a dedicated kitchen garden – or they have an allotment that is some distance from the house. In only a few containers strategically positioned by the back door, it is possible to grow a range of edible plants. Several herbs, small tomatoes and leafy salad crops can even be grown in hanging baskets and window boxes within easy reach.

Health and Hygiene

Some plants can be sensitive to certain bacteria, fungi and viruses that are a normal constituent of garden soil. To avoid the risk of infection, grow them in large plastic containers – which are easy to rinse out with a disinfectant/fungicide before planting – using fresh compost straight from the bag. Vulnerable plants include:

 Cabbages
 Erysimum **(wallflowers)**
 Hosta **(hostas)**
 *Lilium* **(lilies)**
 Tigridia **(tiger flowers)**
 Tomatoes
Tulipa **(tulips)**

Variegated hosta

The Indoor Garden

Containers allow you to grow plants indoors for enjoyment throughout the year, whether it's a tall exotic palm in a hallway or just a few small cacti on a sunny windowsill. If you have a conservatory, you can grow a multitude of different plants. While most houseplants are grown for their foliage, orchids and some others will flower reliably, often for weeks on end.

Anyone who works in an office understands the value of plants. Amongst all the computer equipment, cabling and synthetic grey carpets, they can be used to create small oases of greenery.

Types of Container

Containers are available in a wide range of shapes and sizes – and made from a variety of materials. Choose the appropriate type and size for the plants you wish to grow and the look you are aiming for.

Sourcing Containers

Buy containers in garden centres and DIY stores year-round. Many larger supermarkets also stock containers at key times of year, especially if they also sell plants. For a wider choice, go to plant fairs (which normally take place in spring and summer), where smaller manufacturers and independent artisan makers often showcase their designs. If you are on a budget, or need a lot of pots, containers can usually be found in charity shops, in junk shops and at bring-and-buy sales. Allotment societies and gardening clubs often have quantities of plastic pots for re-use and either give them away free or for a small donation.

Vital Statistics

Take a look at any standard container – the sort used for seed sowing and raising small plants. You'll find that the diameter of the container is the same as the depth – i.e. a container that measures 7.5 cm (3 in) across is also 8 cm (3 in) deep. Nearly all containers have the same proportions – it seems that these suit the majority of plants. Containers that are taller or shallower than the average have specific uses, both in design and plant choice (*see pages 31–33*).

Different Materials

The following types of container are the ones most commonly found in garden centres and homeware stores.

Terracotta

A traditional material for all kinds of pot – a warm buff brown, terracotta is always stylish and ages sympathetically. However, cold weather is the enemy of terracotta. The material is porous, so holds on to water. With a drop in temperature, this freezes and expands, and the container cracks (or even splits) and crumbles around the edge. Frost-resistant terracotta containers are thicker and much heavier than ordinary ones.

Glazed Terracotta

Often made in the Far East and imported, these containers are usually brilliantly coloured. They are often sold in sets of three and are very economical.

Stone

Stone containers lend an air of permanence to any garden, but are heavy to move, so should always be positioned carefully prior to planting. Most stone containers are moulded – cheaper models often have a tell-tale line where two halves have been joined.

Ceramic Pots

Easily breakable, ceramic pots are generally intended for indoor plants. They often have matching saucers to catch excess water (which would otherwise drip on to tables or windowsills). Some pots have no drainage holes. Instead of planting directly into them, use them to conceal a utility plastic pot.

Note: If the container has no holes in the base, regularly empty it of any excess water that has collected at the base.

Plastic and Other Synthetics

Plastic is a lightweight material that is also easy to clean. Some plastic containers are made to look natural, and are so convincing as to be indistinguishable from the real thing. Others are unrepentantly what they are. Plastic does not always age sympathetically – it can discolour and show scratches. Some synthetics are intended for interior use only.

Note: Synthetic pots are sometimes manufactured without drainage holes in the base, so you will have to drill these yourself before planting.

See the Light

Some synthetic containers incorporate light-emitting diodes (LEDs) in the base, so they glow in the dark — often in a range of colours. They are attractive enough to be used with only a simple planting, or even with no plants at all. They look very stylish on a patio that's regularly used for evening entertaining or next to a pool — making magical reflections.

Wood

Wood is frequently used for outdoor planters. Unless treated, wood will swell up and shrink depending on the water content. It may be necessary to treat the material with a wood preservative every year. If allowed to get wet, fungal growths and rots can take hold. Some models have a plastic liner stapled to the inside to prevent moisture from the compost leaching into the wood.

Metal

Metal containers can look very contemporary and stylish and they are often very lightweight. Most have a coating that will guard against rust. Metal dents easily, however, and can lose its shine over time.

Orchid Pots

Many orchids are unlike other plants, in that their roots are adapted to grow in the air (in the wild, many make their home in the branches of trees, clinging on by means of their roots). Orchids are usually sold in clear plastic pots for this reason – their roots do not need to be kept in the dark. You will occasionally find special orchid pots in antique shops. These are made of terracotta but have large holes in the sides – through which the roots can grow.

Weighty Matters

Bear in mind the weight of containers when making your choice. Heavy containers suit heavy plants, such as conifers. If you need to move the plant regularly – for instance an olive tree that you overwinter in a conservatory – a lightweight synthetic may be more practical.

Improvised Containers

Besides the wealth of containers available at garden centres, you can make your own, either for reasons of economy or to fit in with your design ideas.

Good for the Planet

Many gardeners are concerned about the volume of waste packaging that finds its way into landfill sites. However, it is perfectly possible to recycle much of this material – without your garden ending up looking like a scrap heap. Whatever type of recycled container you use, remember to drill holes in the base for drainage before planting. Most can also be customized, as described below. Clear plastic containers are best avoided, however – the roots of nearly all plants need to be kept in the dark. Other possibilities include:

- Paint cans, both plastic and metal
- Old watering cans
- Old boots
- Cooking oil tins
- Biscuit and large sweet boxes, both metal and plastic

Quirky Style

Improvised containers can bring a touch of wit and humour to any garden. For instance, a large olive oil tin could be planted with a small olive tree (or other Mediterranean plant). An old colander (which already has its own drainage holes) can be used for lettuces and other salad crops and herbs. Herbs also look good in wooden or plastic trays (such as are used in supermarkets for fruit and bread). All manner of baskets can be used – either to house smaller plastic pots or lined with black plastic (pierced for drainage) before planting.

Not Time for Tea

If you have a china teapot that has lost its lid, instead of throwing it away, use it for growing a small plant. This will need to be in its own container that just fits in the hole. A planted teapot makes a charming centrepiece for an outside table.

Note:
You will have to remove the plant occasionally to empty out any water that has drained through into the pot – or simply pour it out of the spout.

Customizing Containers

It's easy to bring an individual look to ordinary-looking containers, especially if you find it difficult to source exactly what you want in the usual outlets.

Using Shells, Tiles, Beads and Buttons

Using a flexible spatula, smooth a layer of tile adhesive over the container (this glue type provides a very strong finish that is generally mould resistant). You may need a couple of coats to achieve a suitable depth of adhesive. While this is still wet, press on your chosen decoration. It is easiest to invert the container, and press on the decoration in concentric rings.

Using Paint

Water-based spray paints are easiest to apply. Choose a dry, still, sunny day, if you are working outdoors, or apply the paint in a well-ventilated room. The container should be clean and dry. Several coats may be needed for a good finish.

- **Position:** Invert the container on a cane or short length of bamboo held in place in a bucket of sand.

- **Paint:** As you spray, spin the container round with your other hand to ensure an even coverage.

- **Repeat:** Allow to dry before applying a second coat.

Painting Stripes and Patterns

If you would like to create more exciting paint effects, then why not consider applying horizontal or vertical stripes to your pot:

 Horizontal stripes: Spray on a base coat and allow this to dry (as explained above). Wrap strips of masking tape around the container (or lengths of paper held in position with rubber bands or sticky tape), and then spray with a second colour. Remove the strips once this second coat is dry.

 Vertical stripes: Vertical stripes are trickier, as most containers taper towards the base. Measure the circumference of the top of the container and then divide this by the number of stripes you want (this has to be an even number, otherwise two stripes of the same colour appear side by side). Divide the number of stripes by two. Cut slim rectangles of paper the length of the side of the container and the width of each stripe as it will appear at the top (A). Measure the circumference of the base of the container and then divide this by the number of stripes (this is measurement B). Cut matching triangles from the side of each paper strip that taper to measurement B. Spray the container with your first chosen colour and allow to dry. Attach the strips of paper to the container, spacing them at equal distances, fixing them at top and bottom with masking tape. Spray with the second colour. Remove the strips when the paint is dry.

Patterned effects: Alternatively, decorate the container with stars and/or other shaped stickers before spraying. Peel these off once the paint is dry.

Note: Paint finishes should be regarded as temporary – they will inevitably flake off. To restore the finish, brush off all the old paint with a wire brush, wash the container well, and then leave to dry thoroughly before respraying.

Premature Ageing

It is often said that stone – whether natural or reconstituted – and terracotta age gracefully, developing a patina of lichens and mosses that only adds to their charm. If you have new containers and want to speed this process up, try painting them with sour milk or plain yogurt. This gives these plants a foothold and they will rapidly multiply.

Containers for Specific Plants

While most plants are unfussy as to the type of container you grow them in and are perfectly happy provided they are properly watered and fed, others are more choosy. Some containers are designed with specific plants in mind.

Deep Containers

Some plants are deep-rooted and need an extensive root run if they are to perform to their best. Use deeper than average containers for tomatoes, clematis and sweet peas (*Lathyrus odoratus*). Be sure to water these plants regularly, as the uppermost part of the compost is likely to dry out more rapidly than in a container of conventional dimensions.

Tall and Slender

Large tall containers, up to twice as high as they are wide, always look very stylish and elegant, especially when flanking an imposing doorway or at the edges of a formal pool. But they present the gardener with certain problems:

 They are unstable and likely to fall over.

 A large amount of compost would be needed to fill them.

 It is difficult to know what to plant in them.

The clean lines of this very stylish container are accentuated by the exuberant planting that appears to erupt and flow down the sides.

None of these difficulties is insurmountable, however. These containers do require extra ballast – especially if made of a lightweight polymer. Fill the bottom third with bricks, large stones or rubble. Filling with compost is not a good idea on three counts:

- **It is expensive.**
- **Much will be wasted, as plant roots will not penetrate it.**
- **The volume of compost not occupied with plant roots will become a sump, collecting water that will harbour fungal diseases which may affect plant growth.**

For the best results, after filling the base with ballast material, set a conventional container of the same diameter (or very slightly smaller) in the top, which should nest in unobtrusively. You can then plant this up as normal. Alternatively, use a washing up bowl of the same diameter, in which you have drilled drainage holes and fill this with a number of smaller plants.

Yucca filamentosa

Plants for Tall Containers

Architectural plants always look good in tall containers – they accentuate the elegant line. Alternatively, use several shorter-growing grasses, possibly in a bowl as described above. Tall containers are also ideal for trailing plants whose stems drag on the ground.

- *Agave Americana* **(century plant)**
- *Aloe vera*
- **Buxus/box (clipped to shape)**
- *Clematis* **(less vigorous forms, to trail rather than climb a support)**
- *Eccremocarpus scaber* **(Chilean glory vine)**
- *Festuca glauca*
- *Hedera* **(ivy)**
- *Lobelia* **(trailing forms)**
- *Ophiopogon planiscapus*
- *Pelargonium* **(trailing forms)**
- *Thunbergia alata* **(black–eyed Susan)**
- *Tradescantia* **(trailing forms)**
- *Yucca filamentosa* **(Adam's needle)**

Shallow Pans

Some plants are very shallow-rooted and are adapted to growing in situations where little soil is available – so-called alpines. Grow these plants in pans or troughs filled with gritty compost also topped with grit. Dwarf early bulbs and smaller cacti and succulents also do well in pans.

Plants for shallow pans

Alpines

Alyssum montanum
Aubrieta
Campanula poscharskyana
Gypsophila repens
Phlox drummondii
Saxifraga cotyledon
Thymus (thyme)

Bulbs

Anemone blanda
Crocus
Cyclamen
Muscari (grape hyacinth)
Narcissus/Daffodil (early dwarf forms)
Iris histrioides
Iris reticulata

Campanula poscharskyana

Cacti and succulents

Agave
Aloe
Crassula
Echeveria
Haworthia
Lithops
Mammillaria
Pachyphytum
Rebutia
Sedum

Aloe aristata

What Can I Grow?

It is really amazing the range of plants that can be grown successfully in containers. From tiny alpine plants and bulbs to larger trees and shrubs – there are very few plants that will not do well, given the right compost and size of container.

Choosing Varieties

Look for compact, dwarf or miniature forms of particular plants. These have often been bred specifically for use in containers (or for growing in smaller gardens). Slow-growing plants – such as some conifers – can also be relied on.

Are Any Plants Unsuitable?

Plants that need a lot of water do not usually do well in containers. So-called bog plants, which grow in permanently wet ground, do not develop to their full potential within the confines of a pot.

Fast-growing plants will rapidly outgrow a container so are best avoided. Taller plants often have correspondingly deep root systems to anchor them in the ground and these may also struggle, sometimes pushing roots out through the base holes and into the paving underneath.

Trees, Shrubs and Climbers

These are permanent plants that usually have to be grown in large containers. Confining the roots often has a positive effect – not only does this restrict growth, but it encourages the plant to put its energies into flowering.

Roses

To meet the needs of small gardens, many modern roses are dwarf plants that are ideal for use in pots. But it is also possible to grow larger varieties, with appropriate care and attention.

Bulbs

All bulbs thrive in containers, appreciating the extra drainage and lack of competition from other plants. Some early bulbs are suitable for growing indoors to provide a welcome splash of colour in the depths of winter.

Perennials

Most perennials are border plants, but there are some that you can grow in pots – especially those usually grown for their foliage, such as hostas. This makes slug control much easier.

Grasses

Grasses seem to have been designed for growing in containers – they look stylish over a long period and, being low-maintenance, are ideal for adding life and movement to a paved town garden.

Annuals

These are plants of high summer, producing masses of brilliant flowers. Whether you grow your own from seed or buy bedding plants from the garden centre, fill large containers, hanging baskets and window boxes and enjoy the results over many weeks – even months.

Fruit and vegetables

Many gardeners are surprised at how many edible plants can be grown successfully in containers. Even if you have a paved garden and no allotment, it's possible to enjoy home-grown crops – including nearly all herbs.

Combining plants

Don't imagine you can only grow one type of plant in a single container. It's possible to combine them to create what is effectively a growing flower arrangement. Select plants that have similar requirements in terms of:

 Sun/shade
 Compost type
 Watering
Feeding

Effective combinations are suggested throughout the book.

Sun-loving pelargoniums and daisies will be in flower for many weeks over the summer.

checklist

Plant choice: Decide first of all which plants you actually want to grow. Then find a container – of the appropriate size – that best suits them.

Container: Be creative in your choice of container. If you are having trouble sourcing something, consider making your own or customizing another container.

Material: Make sure the containers you choose are made of materials that best suit your needs.

Proportion: Use containers with unusual proportions – such as tall and narrow – for particular plants. Shallow pans and trays suit early dwarf bulbs, alpines and cacti.

Plant size: When shopping for long-term plants, look out for varieties described as dwarf or miniature or which are known to be slow growing.

Roses: Patio roses have been bred to do well in containers.

Seasons: Use bulbs and annuals for seasonal displays.

Experiment: Container gardening allows you to mix and match plants in a way that would not be possible in the open garden.

Ageing: To age terracotta and stone containers, apply a wash of sour milk or diluted natural yoghurt.

Getting Started

Essential Tools and Equipment

Container gardening has its own range of equipment – some tools that you use in the garden can be commandeered, but, as you are generally working on a smaller scale with containers, some specialist items can be useful.

Hand Tools

A conventional garden trowel can be used for lifting compost and additives such as grit, sand and perlite/vermiculite. Use a handfork for working fertilizer into the upper layer of compost in an already planted container. A handfork is also useful for freeing roots in a compacted rootball and dislodging old compost when repotting and potting on (*see page 68*). Most hand tools are made of metal with wooden, plastic or rubber handles. Plastic versions are lighter and easier to keep clean but can break if subjected to heavy use.

Scoops

Scoops – plastic or metal – in a range of sizes will help you measure out compost. A large scoop holds more than a conventional trowel and the compost is less likely to spill out of it, so many gardeners prefer these. Small scoops are ideal for portioning out powdered or granular fertilizers.

Trays

A large plastic tray, higher at the back edge and with sloping sides, is excellent for mixing compost in. If you are potting up a number of plants, it is easiest to mix up the growing medium in quantity before you start.

Cutting Tools

All-purpose secateurs are suitable for nearly all plants that are grown in containers. For clipping over topiary specimens and other plants with soft stems and leaves, use sheep or topiary shears. Florists' scissors are useful for dead-heading plants and for trimming herbs.

Keeping Tools Clean

Wipe down metal tools with an oily rag after use to lengthen their life. It's also worthwhile cleaning the blades of knives and secateurs before storing them, both to keep them sharp and to prevent rusting.

Gloves

Most gardeners are happy to use their bare hands when working with plants – but there are times when some protection is necessary. Wear stout gloves when handling thorny plants such as roses. If you have sensitive skin, use latex gloves (available at chemists) for bulb planting and if you are going to be in contact with plants known to have poisonous leaves (such as the herb rue, *Ruta graveolens*).

Note: Garden fertilizers and products formulated to combat pests and diseases are legally required to be safe to use, so no protective clothing need be worn.

Watering Equipment

Water is most efficiently delivered to plant roots by means of a watering can. Use without a rose for applying liquid fertilizers direct to the compost. A coarse rose will create a dense shower of heavy drops over plants. If the plants have very delicate leaves, a fine rose is more suitable (and should also be used for seedlings and young bedding plants). Small cans with narrow spouts are used for watering houseplants – some are of very elegant design. Use a spray to mist houseplants, both to raise the humidity and to lower the temperature around them.

Note: Be careful when watering plants with white or very pale flowers. Stray droplets can stain the petals.

Buying Plants

Plants are sold in garden centres, DIY stores and even supermarkets. Florists often sell houseplants (and, sometimes, a limited number of garden plants as well). Nowadays, plants are also sold online.

Choosing Healthy Plants

There's no substitute for going to a garden centre or other retailer and picking out the exact plant that you want – even though you might get a lower price online. To make sure you get the best possible plant:

- **Health:** Check over the top-growth for any signs of pests and diseases – insect eggs are often seen on the undersides of leaves, so make a thorough investigation.

- **Pot-bound:** Upend the plant and examine the base of the pot – if there are roots poking through the drainage holes, the plant is probably pot-bound and will not establish easily.

- **Roots:** If you can, discreetly slide the plant from its container and make sure that all the roots are firm and healthy.

- **Buds:** When buying plants in flower, look to see that there are still plenty of unopened buds – a promise of flowers to come.

Bare-root Plants

Plants are sometimes sold when they are dormant and can be neatly packaged up without any soil. They are usually sold from autumn onwards. Roses and fruit trees and bushes are often sold bare-root (they may resemble little more than a bundle of sticks). Bare-root perennials are usually available in late winter to early spring – daylilies (*Hemerocallis*) and peonies (*Paeonia*) being often sold in this way. Technically, the daffodils, dahlias and begonias that you buy as dry bulbs could be described as bare-root.

In garden centres, bare bulbs are often sold loose, so you can make your own selection – it's usually cheaper to buy them this way.

Shopping Online

Shopping on the internet is quick and simple, but you can't choose the individual plant yourself. Check whether the supplier undertakes to supply only the plants ordered – some may substitute a similar variety if the exact one you want is sold out. Reputable suppliers guarantee their stocks, so a full refund should be payable if the plants fail to thrive. Buying bulbs online is fairly foolproof, as the bulbs are fully dormant and will have been kept in cold storage prior to despatch.

Most live plants survive transit in the postage system remarkably well, assuming they have been packaged correctly. Broken stems need not cause alarm – simply cut them back before planting, and recovery should be brisk.

Did You Know?

Plants were sold mail order well before the advent of the Internet. Most growers are well used to selling plants this way.

Let the Buyer Beware!

Many outlets offer bargain plants in the same way that you would find a sale rail in a clothing store. Tempting though these 'bargains' are, a reduced price label often indicates that the plant has been neglected. Weak-growing, dried-out, pot-bound or diseased plants may not make a good recovery.

Potting Composts

Even experienced gardeners can sometimes be bewildered by the number of different types of potting compost that are available. There are almost as many different sorts of compost as there are containers. Choose the compost that is best suited to the plants you are intending to grow.

Soil-based or Soil-less?

Most composts are based either on soil, made according to formulae devised by the John Innes Institute, or are built on peat, or an alternative. Soil-based composts have a fine texture and drain easily. Soil-less composts tend to be more fibrous.

Soil-based Composts

These comprise a mix of sterilized soil ('loam') and additives such as sand and various plant nutrients. They are heavy but have a very loose open texture. Quality can vary, depending on the batch of soil used in manufacture.

Soil-less Composts

Often sold as 'multi-purpose' composts, these are not graded in the same way. For general use, they have the advantage of being lightweight and very cheap. On the down side, the texture is quite fibrous and the material can form clumps that impede drainage.

The Dreaded Legionnaires' Disease

Rare cases have been reported of outbreaks of Legionnaires' disease associated with the use of potting compost. In storage, bacteria in the compost can multiply to dangerous levels. When opening a new bag of compost, try not to inhale any of the air trapped in the bag. Leave the open bag to stand for half an hour or more (to allow any bacteria to disperse) before using the compost.

John Innes Composts

Soil-based composts are made up according to formulae devised by the John Innes Institute.

- **No.1** is usually used for cuttings and seed sowing.

- **No.2** has slightly more nutrients. Use this for bulbs, annuals and perennials (including grasses and ferns).

- **No.3** has the most nutrients of the lot. This is the ideal compost for permanent plantings of trees, shrubs and bamboos.

Can I use Compost from the Compost Heap?

It is unfortunate that the same term is used for potting compost sold in bags and compost made at home from old plant material and certain organic household waste. This garden compost is unsuitable for use in containers – it contains a wealth of bacterial life that is of huge benefit when added to garden soil but can multiply to toxic levels if used within the confines of a pot. Therefore, only potting compost from a bag – which has been sterilized by the manufacturer – should be used in containers.

Why is Lime an Issue?

All soils (including potting composts) have a degree of acidity/alkalinity. Most potting composts contain some lime – which is alkaline. This is generally beneficial to plant growth, but a few plants such as camellias and heathers are very sensitive and will not grow in a limy medium.

Specialist Composts

The following growing media have been formulated for specific types of plants that have particular needs.

Ericaceous Compost

This type of compost is lime free and thus is suitable for lime-hating plants such as rhododendrons and azaleas, camellias, many heathers and blueberries. These plants will not grow in standard composts. Ericaceous compost is usually based on peat.

Cactus Compost

Cacti are mainly desert plants that are able to survive periods of drought. Cactus compost is therefore very gritty and free-draining, and also low in nutrients.

Orchid Compost

Orchids have a very low nutrient requirement and compost is needed only to stabilize the roots. Most comprise a mix of coarse bark chippings.

Rhododendrons and azaleas thrive in containers and are often used indoors, but they belong to a small group of plants that must have acid compost – in an ordinary compost, the leaves turn yellow.

Additives

The following can be added to compost to improve its drainage and overall performance. They are particularly useful for opening up the texture of multi-purpose composts.

Grit

Horticultural grit is excellent for adding weight to compost – for instance, if you are planting a heavy conifer in a stone or terracotta container. Depending on where it was quarried, it may have a high limestone content – and thus be unsuitable for lime-hating plants. Check the bag before using.

Grit added to compost

Sand

Additions of sand will also add weight to compost. Use it in place of grit for smaller plants and plants with fine root systems. Like grit, it may also be limy.

Perlite

Perlite is a naturally occurring white volcanic glass. It is lightweight and makes an excellent addition to any compost used in situations where excess weight is likely to be an issue – for instance, in containers intended for use on a balcony or roof terrace or for hanging baskets.

Peat, perlite and vermiculite

Can I Use Builder's Sand?

It's best not to use builder's sand (or play pit sand) as an additive to compost. The material is usually very fine grade, so tends to clump, in practice impeding good drainage. It also often contains salts and other minerals that can be detrimental to plants.

Vermiculite

Vermiculite is an expanded mineral, usually beige or grey in colour. It has the same applications as perlite.

Water-retaining Gel

This granular material swells up when wet, delivering water to plant roots without the need for you to water them so often. They are particularly useful for summer containers and hanging baskets, both of which are often in full sun and tend to dry out rapidly.

Food for Thought

Although potting composts already contain a certain amount of plant food, this is rapidly used up by the plants. All plants in containers benefit from supplementary feeding. Adding pelleted fertilizer to compost before use will cut down on the need to feed the plants later on.

Mix it Up

If you are planting a large container – or a number of smaller ones – it's worth mixing a batch of compost in a large bucket or similar. Tip in compost from the bag and then stir in any of the additives mentioned above – about two or three parts of compost to one of the additive. Finally, add any fertilizer and water-retaining gel as necessary. Mix together well with your hands or a trowel.

Drainage Materials

Before filling a container with compost, it's good practice to fill the base (the lowest fifth to quarter of the pot) with some coarse material that will help excess water drain away freely.

Crocks

If you happen to drop and smash a terracotta pot, don't throw it away. The shards are invaluable for use at the base of a pot.

Bricks

Use old and/or broken house bricks, particularly if you need to add ballast – say, to a large container that will be home to a tall plant.

Stones

If you come across large stones when digging in the garden – usually detrimental to plant growth – use them at the base of your containers. These will also improve stability.

Polystyrene

To keep down the ultimate weight of a container, use chunks of polystyrene – such as is commonly used as a packing material for computers and white goods.

Plant Pot Feet

To enable excess water to drain away freely, larger pots should be raised slightly above ground level. Either stand them on special clay 'feet' – three or four around the perimeter of the pot – or on bricks.

Planting Techniques

Whether you are planting a single plant in a large container or using several, the procedure is the same. Hanging baskets and window boxes are each planted in a slightly different way.

Containers

A brand new container needs no particular preparation – though some gardeners believe that soaking a terracotta pot in water before planting will prevent the potting compost drying out too quickly after planting.

Water: First, water the plant (or plants) you will be using – this will consolidate the compost around the rootball, making the plant easier to handle. Leave to drain.

Drainage: Line the base of the container with suitable drainage material, making sure the drainage holes are covered (so that compost is not washed out of the container when you water).

Compost: Begin to fill with compost to cover the drainage material. Lightly firm this down with your hands.

Plant up: Set the plant (or main plant) in the middle of the container to check the planting depth. Once planted, the surface of the compost should be 2–2.5 cm (¾ –1 in) below the rim of the pot to allow for watering. Add more compost to the base of the container as necessary.

Backfill: With the plant in position, begin to backfill with the potting mix. Add any further plants around the perimeter as you go.

Water in: Once planted, water well from a watering can fitted with a fine rose. Allow to drain. Once the compost has settled, you can see if you need to add any more compost to make a level surface if the water has caused some dips to appear here and there.

Note: When firming compost, take care not to press too hard. This can compact the surface, so water will settle on the top without draining quickly.

Good Hygiene

If you are reusing a container that has already had plants in it, wash it out thoroughly before use. Old bits of compost clinging to the sides may be harbouring fungal and other diseases (or the eggs of certain pests). Rinse and scrub the containers under running water, then allow to dry before planting up.

Use bedding plants or other small plants in window boxes. When planting, allow a small gap between the compost surface and the edge of the box, so the compost won't wash away when you water.

Window Boxes

Window boxes are available in the same range of materials as conventional containers. They are usually used for embellishing house fronts and for creating seasonal displays. Nothing gives a property more kerb appeal than a few smart window boxes. The important thing to remember is that if a window box is on an upper level of a building, it must be properly secured to avoid accidents.

Plant up the box in the same way as for a conventional container (see page 50), but bear in mind that a window box is normally viewed from only one side – like a stage set. Trailing plants such as ivy always look good at the front, as they have plenty of room to cascade down. Complete the cast with a few more upright-growing plants at the back.

Top Tip

To fix a window box in position, either chain it at the sides to the frame of the window or screw it to the windowsill. Raise the box on small chocks of wood (through which you can drill) to ensure good drainage and to prevent water collecting on the sill.

Smartening up a Window Box

Most garden centres sell decorative low fencing (made of wicker, bamboo, timber or plastic) in short sections – intended to edge a garden path or mark beds in a potager. Nail or screw a section to the side of a cheap plastic window box for a stylish finish.

Winter Interest

Nothing brightens up a house more in winter than a few colourful shrubs and bulbs in a window box. Because plants do not grow much in winter, you do not actually have to plant the box in the conventional way. Buy small plants and bulbs in containers and then simply arrange them as they are in the box. Fill in the gaps between the containers with compost or moss. When you water, water each container individually. In spring, either discard the plants or put them out in the garden (or pot them on into bigger containers for use elsewhere). You can then plant up the window box for summer interest.

Pernettya berries

Plants for a Winter Window Box

Buxus (box)

Crocus

Cyclamen

Dwarf conifers

Erica/Heather (winter-flowering)

Euonymus

Hedera (ivy)

Helleborus (hellebore)

Narcissus/Daffodil (early dwarf forms)

Pernettya

Skimmia (for flower buds and berries)

Cyclamen ready
for planting

Hanging Baskets

Hanging baskets are nearly always used to provide a mass of colourful flowers in summer. They are usually made of plastic-coated wire that has to be lined before planting. For maximum impact, cram as many plants as you can into the basket – normal recommendations about spacing plants do not apply. To make the job easier, rest the unplanted basket on the rim of a bucket or container. Plant your hanging basket as follows:

Line: Line the basket with moss or a hanging basket liner.

Moss: If you are using moss to retain the compost, cut a large circle of black plastic (an old compost bag is ideal) to fit inside the liner.

Cut: With scissors or a sharp knife, cut holes or slits in the plastic at the base for drainage.

Compost: Fill the basket about one-third full with compost. Lightly press this down with your fingers.

Sides: Begin to plant the sides of the container. Make slits in the liner, then push the rootballs through so they rest on the compost layer.

Top: Add further compost to cover the rootballs and then plant the top of the container. For a strong effect, choose one central plant that will dominate – such as a fuchsia or pelargonium – with smaller, trailing plants around the edge.

Potting Compost

Bearing in mind that a fully planted basket – especially after watering – will be heavy, it is best to use a lightweight compost. You can either buy a ready-mixed one or make your own, using multi-purpose compost but replacing a third with perlite or vermiculite. Add fertilizer pellets (see page 66) and water-retaining gel. Work these into the compost thoroughly with a hand fork before you begin planting.

Water-retaining Gel

These powdered gels can be a life-saver for plants in hanging baskets (and for other container plants). Stir a few teaspoons of the dry granules into the compost. Once wet, they swell up and deliver moisture gradually, reducing – but not eliminating – the need to water. Make sure the granules are evenly dispersed – clumps will set in the compost, exactly like a jelly (jello).

Top Tip

For even growth, turn the basket at weekly intervals – otherwise the plants will all grow (and flower) towards the sun.

Hanging the Basket

Baskets are normally hung on brackets firmly screwed to house walls. Make sure that the bracket projects far enough out from the wall to accommodate the basket's radius plus the overhanging plants. Hang up the basket and then water well.

Did You Know?

If you use moss to line a hanging basket, it will carry on growing provided you keep up the watering.

Decorative Trims

Though it is not strictly necessary, you can add style to any container planting by covering the compost surface with a decorative mulch.

Bark Chips

Bark chips make a suitable mulch for woodland plants such as shade-loving hostas and ferns. It also works well with shrubs and roses in containers.

Grit

Grit makes an excellent trim for all sorts of plants. But if they are lime-haters (see page 46), make sure the grit has not been quarried from a limestone source. It looks particularly good with Mediterranean plants, alpines and dwarf bulbs.

Marble Chippings

These look very stylish as a trim for large containers placed next to the front door. Usually white, they reflect light back on to the plants in a very flattering way. If you are using them long-term, you will probably need to remove and wash them periodically to remove any traces of green algal growth (which can appear if they are allowed to stay wet over a period).

Sea Shells

Use sea shells to give your containers a nautical feel. They are particularly effective used around coastal plants – scrubby plants such as Mediterranean pines and sea holly.

Glass Beads

These are often used indoors to add colour and interest to green-leaved foliage plants. They can also be used on outdoor containers, but may lose some of their lustre after prolonged exposure to the elements.

Stay Cool

Besides looking attractive, a mulch can also be of great practical value. It prevents water from evaporating from the uppermost compost layer, thus keeping roots cool. That can also mean less watering. But it's a good idea to push a finger through the mulch periodically to check that the compost has not dried out completely.

Keep Trims Smart

Almost inevitably, any trim you use will wash through into the compost below with repeated waterings. You can prevent this as follows: Cut a circle from a length of horticultural fleece or membrane (these materials are perforated to allow water to pass through), the same circumference as the container. Make a slit through to the centre, where you can cut a hole of suitable size for the stem of the plant. Place this on the compost surface before topping with the trim.

Pedestals, Stands and Etagères

You can raise containers on pedestals, stands and etagères in order to bring the plants up to eye level. They are often highly decorative in their own right. Trailing plants work particularly well, as their stems can be allowed to hang downwards, well below the pot.

Pedestals

Pedestals are generally of some architectural value. In the garden, they are usually cast in concrete (unless sculpted more classically from blocks of marble or granite) and are particularly effective in combination with decorative urns. Architectural plants such as aeoniums, agaves, phormiums and yuccas are always doubly striking when raised on a pedestal.

A container on a pedestal is bound to be a strong feature in any garden. Use one as a focal point at the end of a path, to mark the centre of a circular garden (for instance, a herb wheel in a potager) or just to raise the eye and give style to a border of mixed plants. In pairs, they can flank a path or doorway or herald a flight of steps. Wooden pedestals and lightweight models made of plastic and other synthetics are generally intended for use in the house.

If you do not think there is much room for plants, use shelves or even a step ladder to make full use of available space – most plants have a good head for heights.

Stands

Stands are of open construction, generally made of metal (or wood for indoor use), and may incorporate shelves. Use these for single plants. The shelves allow you to grow more plants in the available ground space – two, three or more plants will occupy the same area as a single plant. Bear in mind that the upper plant or plants will shade the lower ones, so these should be types that are tolerant of less light.

Etagères

Usually made of metal – and sometimes of elaborate design – étagères will hold a number of plants. Some are intended to stand or lean against a wall, while others are free-standing. You can even find models that fit into a corner, which are ideal for use on a balcony. Etagères comprise a series of shelves, usually slatted for drainage, and are often larger towards the base.

Tips on Watering

 Make sure that you can easily water plants that are at or above eye level – or choose drought-tolerant types.

 Plants in an étagère will need watering individually – it is tempting just to water from the top, but plants lower down may not receive their fair share.

checklist

Tools: Consider investing in some new tools that will make planting and routine maintenance more of a pleasure, particularly if you have many plants in containers. A coarse and a fine rose for fitting on the spout of your watering can would be a good investment.

Gloves: Wear gloves if you have sensitive skin or whenever you are handling thorny plants.

Potting compost: Choose composts carefully, bearing in mind the needs of the plants you want to grow. Most plants will be perfectly happy in any compost, but some have very specific requirements – for instance, lime-hating plants must have ericaceous compost.

Additives: Decide whether you'll get better results by adding anything to the compost, such as grit or additional fertilizer – the improvement in plant performance can be striking.

Hygiene: Thoroughly clean any old pots before using them again.

Drainage: Before planting, make sure you have some suitable drainage material to hand – few plants like sitting with their roots in wet compost.

Trims: Decorative trims can make a huge difference to the overall appearance of a plant.

Display: Would any look best displayed on a pedestal or étagère? Raising plants above ground level can be a good way of making the best use of limited space.

Care & Maintenance

Watering

All plants need water for good growth. Garden soil usually stays moist enough to satisfy the needs of most plants – but compost in containers dries out, so regular watering is always necessary.

When to Water

Plants need water most when they are growing strongly, usually throughout spring and summer. The compost should be kept just moist and not allowed to dry out. At the height of summer, you may need to water some containers (especially hanging baskets) twice a day.

Surprisingly, you should check the compost in all your containers even after it's been raining. Some container plants develop a leaf canopy that's broader than the container's circumference, effectively screening the compost surface from rainfall – so the compost stays dry. So you may need to water even after a summer shower.

A water butt positioned near your containers will prove very useful during dry periods.

Water Conservation

Water is a precious resource, which is sometimes in limited supply during summer droughts. Make the maximum use of it as follows:

 Water butts: Install water butts attached to guttering to collect rainwater from roofs.

Keep plants cool by moving them to a shady area during hot weather.

'Grey' water: Collect water from domestic use (washing machines, baths, showers and washbasins) for recycling – known as 'grey' water.

Watering cans: Water plants in containers individually using a watering can, not by spraying over them with a hosepipe (which wastes water – there may even be a ban on hosepipe use in your area).

Timing: Water in the evening, rather than the morning. Less water will be lost through evaporation, so more is available to the plants.

Microclimate: In hot weather, group plants in containers together in a shady area to create a 'microclimate'. The air around the leaves will stay humid, helping to keep the plants cool.

Reviving Neglected Plants

If your plants dry out completely and the leaves are wilting – perhaps because you have been away during a period of hot dry weather – they can generally be revived as follows:

Move the plants into a cool shady area.

Stand the containers in a bucket or trough of water (note: the water should reach to just below the compost level – otherwise surface compost will float free).

When the compost is fully moistened and the leaves of the plant are firm again, lift each plant from the water and allow to drain.

Feeding

Since composts contain only limited amounts of plant nutrients, supplementary feeding is necessary, particularly for permanent plantings of trees and shrubs.

What is Plant Food?

Plants need three major elements (macronutrients) for good growth. Plant fertilizers contain these in differing proportions (these are always stated on the label). Use a nitrogen-high fertilizer in spring to promote a rush of new leaves. Potassium-high fertilizers – applied from mid-spring onwards – will help develop flowers and fruits. Plants use the three elements for the following purposes:

- ✓ **Nitrogen (N) for healthy bright green leaves**
- ✓ **Potassium (K) to help develop flowers and fruit**
- ✓ **Phosphorus (P) to promote root growth**

Phosphorus promotes healthy roots

Types of Fertilizer

Pelleted and granular fertilizers can be added to compost before use, or can be lightly worked into the compost surface with a hand fork. Some plant foods are made up as clusters of pellets, for pushing into the compost surface as required.

Fertilizers provide plants with nutrients they need for good growth. Always apply them in the dosage recommended by the manufacturer.

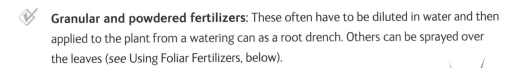

Granular and powdered fertilizers: These often have to be diluted in water and then applied to the plant from a watering can as a root drench. Others can be sprayed over the leaves (*see* Using Foliar Fertilizers, below).

Liquid fertilizers: These are much faster-acting than dry ones, as the dissolved nutrients are immediately available to the plants. But some of the product is inevitably lost through drainage. Liquid fertilizers are often sold ready formulated in bottles fitted with a spray. These are very convenient to use, as you do not need to bother with measuring out the appropriate quantity of water.

When to Feed

Feed plants when they are growing strongly in spring and summer. Feeding in autumn/winter, when they are resting, is unnecessary.

Using Foliar Fertilizers

Foliar fertilizers, sprayed directly over the leaves, are excellent for giving a quick boost to plants that have just suffered a setback – for instance, if you have had to cut off diseased stems or have treated them for a pest attack. So that the product does not blow about – which is wasteful – spray during still weather. Spray either in the evening or on a dull day – strong sunlight can scorch wetted leaves. Spray the undersides as well as the upper surfaces of the leaves for maximum effectiveness.

Potting On and Repotting

If you are keeping a plant in a container long-term – for instance, a bay tree by the front door – you will need either to transplant it into increasingly large pots as it grows or replace some of the compost periodically to keep it fresh.

When to Do It

You will need to pot on a plant when it has outgrown the pot it is in – when the roots fill the container. Tilt the pot and check the drainage holes – if you can see the tips of the roots showing through, it is time to pot on. Potting on is best done in mid-spring or when the plant has just finished flowering.

Top Tip

When potting on, choose a container the next size up. It is not good for a plant with a small rootball to sit in too large a container. The large volume of compost around the roots will act as a sump, holding water that can rapidly become a breeding ground for harmful fungi and bacteria. If you pot into only the next size up, the roots will rapidly grow out to fill the container, so this problem will not occur.

Potting On

This is a routine task that you need to do annually until the plant has reached the desired size, as follows:

- **Compost:** Water the plant first to consolidate the compost around the roots and then allow it to drain.

- **Remove the plant:** Slide the plant from the container. Running a knife around the edge of the rootball can help you ease it free.

- **Roots:** Lightly tease out the roots with your fingers, if they have started to coil round.

- **New pot:** Pot up the plant in a container the next size up, using the appropriate compost.

- **Water:** Water the plant well.

Repotting

Once a plant has reached full size – or it has grown as large as you want it to – repot it annually in spring to keep it fresh and vigorous:

- **Rootball:** Water the plant well to consolidate the rootball.

☑ **Remove the plant**: Slide the plant from the container, using a sharp knife to help you, if necessary.

☑ **Clean**: Wash off all the old compost from the roots under running water.

☑ **Trim**: Depending on the thickness of the roots, give them a light trim with secateurs or scissors.

☑ **Hygiene**: Wash out the container thoroughly.

☑ **Repot**: Return the plant to its container, filling with the appropriate compost.

☑ **Water**: Water the plant well.

Troubleshooting

Some plants – such as agapanthus and clivias – actually thrive when the roots are congested, so should only be repotted when absolutely necessary and the roots seem to be bursting from the pot. Soak the containers in a bucket of water for several hours to free the roots. Sometimes these plants can become so congested that you have to cut or break the container in order to get the plant out.

Clivia

Agapanthus

Glazed terracotta pots present a related problem. If they are bulbous in shape, it can be very difficult to remove the rootball intact. In this case, take a long sharp knife and cut straight down around the perimeter of the pot and through the roots. Many plants actually thrive after this apparently brutal treatment – it encourages them to put out new roots.

Top-dressing

If a plant has reached its desired size and is now in a large container, it may be impractical to repot it regularly. To keep the plant healthy and growing strongly, top-dress it as follows:

- **Sheeting**: Lay a length of plastic sheeting or newspaper on the ground next to the plant.

- **Position**: Carefully tilt the container over the sheeting.

- **Remove**: With your fingers, scrape out as much of the compost from the surface as you can.

- **Compost**: With the container back in an upright position, add fresh compost (with added grit or sand and fertilizer as appropriate) to restore the level.

- **Water**: Water well and then add a further dressing of grit or bark, as appropriate.

Note: Rather than discarding the spent compost, it can be added to the compost heap.

Providing Support

Plants with tall and/or flexible stems need to be supported. There are a variety of options, some of which will be hidden by the plant's top-growth, others being attractive in their own right.

Trellis Panels

Climbing plants in large containers can be positioned against walls and fences, then the stems can be trained on trellis panels attached to the wall or fence.

Trellis Obelisks

Large free-standing containers – as long as they are heavy enough not to blow over in strong winds – can even accommodate trellis obelisks. Use these for climbing roses and clematis. Most are attractive enough to be a feature even when the plants are dormant in winter.

Wigwams

For a smaller, more informal support, position three to five slim canes or bamboos around the edge of the container, then tie them at the top with stout string or wire. For additional support, run lengths of wire or horticultural twine in a spiral up the wigwam.

Look Out!

Serious eye injuries can be caused by bamboo canes protruding through plants in the garden. Plastic stoppers are available that fit over the ends of the canes to reduce the risk. Alternatively, mould balls of modelling clay in your fingers and press them on to the exposed ends.

Chicken Wire

To support sweet peas and other annual climbers and shorter-growing clematis, you can simply wrap a length of chicken wire around the container, wiring it closed. The plants will rapidly cover the support.

Top Tip

To avoid damaging delicate roots, position the support in the container before adding the plants.

Climbers for Containers

In general, climbers are vigorous plants – but there are several less rampant ones that do well in containers. Always choose a large container.

Clematis
'Bijou'
'Dancing Queen'
'Fireworks'
'Mercury'
'Silver Moon'
'Violet Charm'
'Warsaw Nike'
Eccremocarpus scaber (Chilean glory vine)
Hedera helix (small-leaved ivy)
Ipomoea (morning glory)
Lathyrus odoratus (sweet pea)
Thunbergia alata (black-eyed Susan)

Sweet pea

Climbers are natural woodland plants. Although many will do well in full sun, most are happiest with some shelter from direct light at the hottest time of the day. It is particularly important to keep roots cool by positioning containers where they will be shaded in summer.

Pruning and Dead-heading

Plants in containers need pruning and dead-heading in the same way as plants in the garden. Pruning restricts the size of a plant, while dead-heading keeps them flowering.

Routine Maintenance

Good gardeners always have a pair of secateurs handy. Be ready to snip away any damaged, diseased or dead growth as soon as you spot it. Variegated plants (with coloured leaf margins) have a tendency to throw out plain green shoots periodically. These are always very vigorous and spoil the appearance of the plant. Cut them back straight away.

Lightly Clipped

Permanent plantings of evergreen shrubs – box (*Buxus*), privet (*Ligustrum*), bay (*Laurus nobilis*) and dwarf conifers – can be given a light trim in spring and summer (and any other time when you want to spruce them up) with topiary shears (or sheep shears, which are the same thing). These are fun and easy to use but will only cut very soft young growth – for a harder prune, you need secateurs.

Bulbs

If you want to keep bulbs from year to year – rather than discarding them after flowering – remove the flowers as they fade. This prevents the plant from forming seed, which wastes its energies. Feed the plants for as long as the leaves stay green, then allow them to turn yellow and die back naturally (when you should stop watering and feeding). This builds up the bulb for good flowering the next year.

Annuals

To ensure that annuals keep producing flowers, remove faded flowers regularly. This prevents them from setting seed, which expends the plants' energies. It should be possible to keep annuals flowering until they literally die from exhaustion.

As flowers start to fade, remove them to prevent the plant from making seed. Cut just below the base of the flower and allow the stem to die back naturally to build up the bulb's food store.

Grooming Grasses

Most grasses tend to accumulate a certain amount of dead material. Not only is this unsightly, but it prevents the new leaves from growing strongly. In spring, run your fingers through the grass, pulling out the old leaves (which should come away freely from the base of the plant).

Some grasses have tough blade-like leaves that can cut skin. Wear stout gloves when handling these – you may also need a sharp knife, scissors or secateurs to cut out some older growth.

A really good pair of secateurs and gloves are at the top of every gardener's wish list.

A Little TLC

After an attack with secateurs or shears, plants pause for breath, then make a recovery — either by putting out fresh new leaves or building a second crop of flowers. But pruning and dead-heading inevitably set them back, so to make sure of a brisk response, feed them well. If you have pruned evergreen plants, a seaweed feed will encourage new leaves. For further flowers on summer annuals, use a diluted tomato or hanging-basket fertilizer.

What Not to Dead-head

Some shrubs are grown for their decorative autumn fruits, and these should not be dead-headed — the flowers should be allowed to fade on the plant. Pyracanthas have red, yellow or orange berries. Some ground-cover roses have bright red hips. If you grow sweet peas (*Lathyrus odoratus*), it's sometimes worth allowing a few seedheads to develop in late summer to provide seed for new plants next year.

Pyracantha berries

Overwintering

Plants in containers need particular care over winter if they are to survive the worst of the weather. With their roots above ground level, they are always more vulnerable to frost. If the roots are allowed to freeze, the plant may die.

Moving Plants

Put small plants (including seedlings and cuttings) in a cold frame. Keep the frame open during mild periods. During very cold weather, cover the frame with a thick blanket or piece of old carpet. Leave this in place during the day if the temperature stays below freezing.

Tender plants growing in pots, such as sago palms (*Cycas revoluta*), should be moved inside during the winter months (unless they are too heavy to move easily).

Hardy plants need the minimum additional protection – simply moving them close to the house walls whenever a cold spell is forecast can

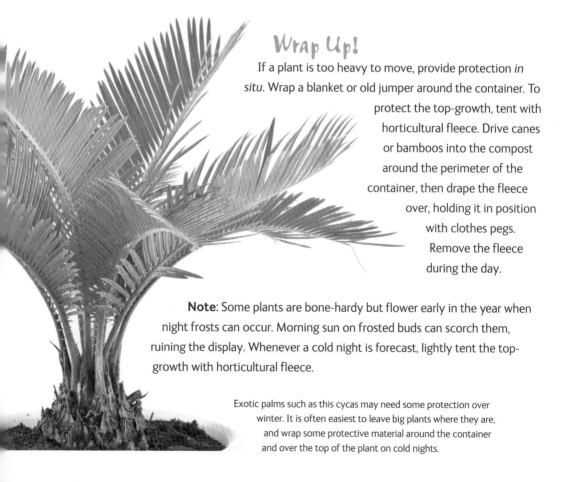

be sufficient to keep off the worst of the cold. For additional protection, bring them into an unheated greenhouse, carport or porch.

Another ploy, where this is possible, is to dig a hole in a spare patch of soil, then sink the plant in its container into this (the compost surface should be level with the soil). If you have a paved garden and nowhere to store the plants, simply drop each container into a second one the next size up, so there is effectively a double layer around the roots.

Wrap Up!

If a plant is too heavy to move, provide protection *in situ*. Wrap a blanket or old jumper around the container. To protect the top-growth, tent with horticultural fleece. Drive canes or bamboos into the compost around the perimeter of the container, then drape the fleece over, holding it in position with clothes pegs. Remove the fleece during the day.

Note: Some plants are bone-hardy but flower early in the year when night frosts can occur. Morning sun on frosted buds can scorch them, ruining the display. Whenever a cold night is forecast, lightly tent the top-growth with horticultural fleece.

Exotic palms such as this cycas may need some protection over winter. It is often easiest to leave big plants where they are, and wrap some protective material around the container and over the top of the plant on cold nights.

Some Special Cases

A couple of architectural, tropical-looking plants such as banana palms and tree ferns have become popular in recent years. They are not reliably hardy in all areas but, being large plants, can be difficult to move. You can protect them in the following ways:

 Banana palms: Wait until the first hard frost has blackened all the foliage, then cut or strip this off to leave a bare stem (larger specimens may have several stems). Encircle the stem or stems with a length of chicken wire, sinking this into the compost surface. Pack this cylinder loosely with dry straw. The straw should reach above the tops of the stems. Cover the top with a plastic sheet to keep off the wet.

 Tree ferns: Place a collar of chicken wire around the trunk and loosely pack this with dry straw. Leave the fronds at the top of the stem to die back naturally. If the weather turns very cold, pack straw loosely over the top of the plant.

Note: The straw you use for insulation must be absolutely dry. Take care not to pack too tightly – the aim is to keep the plants dry over winter, so good air circulation through the material is essential.

Make an insulating duvet for banana palms by wrapping a length of chicken wire around the plant, then stuffing this with dry straw – cosy.

Pests and Diseases

Plants in containers are subject to the same pests and diseases as other plants. In some respects, they are more vulnerable – but on the plus side, they are usually easy to control.

Slugs

Slugs are among the worst garden pests, as they will feed on the soft young growth of virtually any plant. They have no problem climbing up the sides of containers to devour emerging hostas and dahlias, among others.

Top Tip

Slug pellets and other poisons are best avoided in containers – they actually attract the pests.

Control: Pick the slugs off by hand, in the evening and after rainfall, when they are active. Check the undersides of containers – where they are often to be found lurking – and flick them off. Protect vulnerable plants with lengths of copper tape stuck around the perimeter of the containers. The copper reacts with their mucus, giving them an electric shock.

Vine Weevil

This wingless pest affects potentially all plants in containers. The adults, which are active in summer, actually cause little damage apart from nibbling at the edges of leaves. The real villains are the grubs, which emerge from eggs laid by the females on the compost surface, then tunnel down. They overwinter in the compost, feeding on plant roots. As the plant is dormant then, you may not realize you have a problem till you come to repot it in spring.

Control: The grubs are easily controlled by the use of a parasitic nematode (a microscopic organism that eats the pest from the inside). If you spot damage to the leaves, treat the compost over the following weeks to eliminate the emerging grubs.

Aphids

This is a generic term that covers a range of insect pests including greenfly and blackfly. They are usually active in spring, clustering on stems, leaves and buds, from which they suck sap.

Control: Spray the pest with an insecticide as soon as you spot them or dislodge them with a strong jet of water from a hose.

Parasitic Nematodes

These microscopic organisms are increasingly used to control pests. They are generally sold dormant as a compound that has to be dissolved in water before use. Once watered into the compost, they become active and start to feed on the pests and breed. Several applications are usually necessary to eradicate the pest entirely.

Leaf Spots

Yellow, brown or black spots on leaves are generally caused by a range of fungi. Spotting can affect plants in spring and summer, often during damp weather.

Control: Cut off all affected leaves, then spray the plant with a fungicide. Boost recovery with liquid or foliar feed.

Grey Mould/Botrytis

A grey, fluffy mould often appears on plants, particularly if growth is congested. The disease proliferates in wet conditions and is easily passed from plant to plant.

Thoroughly spraying plants with a fungicide will deal with many leaf problems. Spray to wet the plant thoroughly, also paying attention to the undersides of leaves.

Control: Cut back all affected growth, then spray with a fungicide. Make sure adjacent plants do not touch each other. Prune out congested stems.

Physiological Problems

Many plant problems are caused simply by poor growing conditions – too much, or too little, water, frost and sudden fluctuations in temperature. These factors can cause leaves to discolour and fall from the plant, weakening it and making it more vulnerable to disease.

Keep plants growing strongly by watering well (without overwatering), applying suitable fertilizers and protecting them from extremes of weather.

checklist

- **Water:** Water plants frequently when they are in full growth in spring and summer. Water less during autumn and winter (though most should not be allowed to dry out completely). Check the compost regularly to assess the water content – it should always feel slightly damp.

- **Feed:** Feed plants with an appropriate fertilizer when they are growing strongly. Use a foliar feed to give them a quick start.

- **Pot on/repot:** Pot on or repot plants when their roots fill the container. If you do not want them to grow any bigger, trim the roots before returning them to the same container (or to one of the same size).

- **Top-dress:** Top-dress plants that are too unwieldy to pot on or repot.

- **Support:** Provide support for any plant that needs it.

- **Prune:** Clip over plants, as necessary, to keep them neat. Remove dead foliage from grasses in spring to make way for fresh new growth.

- **Dead-head:** Remove the faded flowers from bulbs. Dead-heading annuals (and many other plants) will prolong the flowering period.

- **Protect:** Provide winter protection for any plant that needs it.

- **Pests and diseases:** Check plants regularly for signs of pests and diseases, and deal with any problem promptly.

Container
Designs

Creating A Look

With such a wide range of styles of container available to suit all budgets, it's possible to create a range of different looks. Choose the type that best fits in with the rest of the garden – formal, cottage-style, minimalist – and the plants to match.

An Integrated Look

For the most harmonious effect, restrict your use of materials. Choose just one type of pot – in different sizes for each plant or plant combination – that matches or chimes with materials already in the garden. If you have a lot of decking and fencing, for instance, wooden planters extend the theme. Stone and terracotta always work well with concrete paving.

Terracotta – brick red or pale buff – works well in a range of settings, as it's a traditional, neutral material that stands up to the elements and always looks attractive.

Eclectic Tastes

Some gardeners prefer to take a more relaxed approach to design and are more than happy to mix and match a range of different containers (and plants). Some may be chosen for personal or sentimental reasons – for instance, you may have inherited one particular container and bought another as a souvenir when on holiday. Gardens that combine a broad range of containers always have a particular charm of their own.

Stone and Terracotta

Since these materials age sympathetically, they give a garden an air of maturity and permanence. They work well in gardens next to older, established houses and buildings. Use them for long-term plantings of trees, shrubs, climbers and roses.

Antique Style

Reclamation yards and some specialist antique shops sell old stone containers (and other ornaments), if you are looking for something unusual. Alongside these, you may find old kitchen sinks, horse troughs and other animal feeders that can be used for growing plants. Country house auctions are also happy hunting grounds for collectors.

Glazed Terracotta

Reflecting their oriental origins, these always look good in an oriental-themed garden. They lend themselves to oriental plants such as Japanese maples (*Acer japonicum* and *A. palmatum*), hostas, bamboos and the Japanese painted fern, *Athyrium nipponicum* 'Pictum'. Since the finish is often glossy and brilliantly coloured, they bring a jewel-like accent to predominantly green plantings in shady spots.

Wooden Half-barrels

Barrels always looks good in a relaxed country setting. They are ideal for a flamboyant mix of spring-flowering bulbs and bedding plants or for summer plantings of annuals, fuchsias and pelargoniums. In the longer term, they particularly suit hydrangeas and other small flowering shrubs.

Plastic

While plastic is often little more than a utility material, it always looks fresh and is easy to keep clean, not to mention being inexpensive, readily available and light in weight. Use plastic pots in a contemporary setting or near a newly built property where the paving is still in pristine condition and has yet to weather down.

Metal

Metal is an ideal material for a minimalist, high-tech design, perhaps in a city garden where the focus is on strong lines and proportion and less so on the actual plants. Reflecting the light, metal often works best with a discreet planting, as it's usually the container itself that catches the eye.

Match the Planting to the Pot

Decide whether it's the container or the plants in it that are to be the focus of attention. A very elaborate moulded container in the Classical style works best with a very simple planting – such a container can often look good even without any plants at all. Conversely, use very simple containers for riotous plantings of mixed summer annuals.

Cutting-edge Design

For a really stylish look, try planting grasses in a geometric planter. Cut the plants sharply across on the horizontal (possibly applying the golden section, *see* page 91). Alternatively, use box plants severely clipped to a firm shape.

Fatsia japonica

Hosta

Architectural Plants

The following plants all make a bold statement:

Agave americana (century plant)

Cordyline

Cycas revoluta (Japanese sago palm)

Dicksonia antarctica (Australian tree fern)

Dracaena

Fatsia

Hosta

Musa basjoo (banana palm)

Opuntia (prickly pear)

Phoenix canariensis (date palm)

Phormium (New Zealand flax)

Trachycarpus fortunei (Chusan palm)

Yucca gloriosa (Spanish dagger)

Palm

Note: Several so-called architectural plants have spiky pointed leaves or leaf edges that can cut like knives. Be careful when handling these plants and be cautious about where you put them – injuries are best avoided, especially if the garden is also a play area for small children.

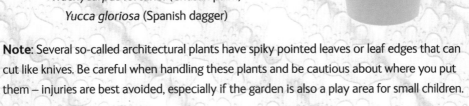

A Sense of Proportion

A fundamental aspect of all design is the use of proportion. Even very simple plantings can be highly effective if due consideration is given to size and placement. Since containers are so easy to move around, have fun experimenting to see where and what combinations work best.

If there's a particular container you like, use more of the same to create unity within the garden.

Grouping Containers

For informal groups, use odd numbers of containers. A bold group – possibly using similar containers in a range of sizes – always looks better and more generous than isolated containers dotted around. For a formal look, use even numbers of similarly sized containers placed at regular intervals, say, to punctuate the edges of a border or to flank a path. These will give a sense of rhythm to the garden, even if the flower beds themselves are informally planted. If you have a formal square or rectangular pool, place large containers at each corner to highlight the geometry.

A single large container can make an impressive focal point – for instance, at the end of a path or in the centre of a lawn.

Containers that have a strong visual appeal in their own right, can be effective even when unplanted – in isolation, they can make a bold statement, as this glazed jar demonstrates.

The Golden Section

The golden section (or golden ratio) is found throughout the natural world and is widely used in architecture and classical painting, sculpture and graphic design. In essence, it involves breaking a line into two unequal parts so that the proportion between the shorter and the longer part is the same as that between the longer and the whole line. In practice, this leads to a ratio of (roughly) 1:1.6 or (in whole numbers) 5:8 – proportions that are always pleasing to the eye. (As with *pi*, the exact value of the ratio can never be precisely calculated.)

When arranging containers, the spaces in between them can be as important visually as the containers themselves – what designers often refer to as 'volumes and voids'.

How to Use the Golden Section

Use the golden section whenever you need to divide up a space or if you need to decide on a suitably sized container for a particular height of plant. For instance, if you are planting a clipped box obelisk that measures 40 cm (16 in) high, choose a 25 cm (10 in) container. As another example, if you are placing containers along the edge of a path and the path is 1 m (3 ft) wide, place the containers 1.6 m (4 ft 10 in) apart.

Note: The principles of proportion outlined here are in no way hard-and-fast rules. You should always be guided by what strikes you as balanced and harmonious and what works best in the garden. Practical considerations often take precedence.

Using the 3:5 ratio greatly enhances the appeal of even the simplest of plantings.

The Fibonacci Sequence

This is a sequence of numbers, each consecutive one of which is the sum of the preceding two, as follows: 0 1 1 2 3 5 8 13 21 34, etc.

To use these, choose two adjacent numbers (ignoring zero) and then base your proportions on these. Floral designers often use the 2:3 ratio when arranging flowers in a vase – the part of the tallest stem visible above the rim of the vase would be one-and-a-half times the vase's height. Applying this to containers, a box obelisk measuring 37.5 cm (15 in) would be a pleasing size for a 25 cm (10 in) pot. You can, of course, reverse the ratios – reversing the 3:5 ratio, if you have a tall container 60 cm (24 in) high, plant it with a box ball 36 cm (approximately 15 in) high.

In practice, Fibonacci numbers can be simpler to apply than the golden section. (The further you go down the sequence, the closer to the golden section you get.) But as with all aspects of design, don't be afraid to break the rules occasionally.

Note: The 1:1 proportion is always very strong and should be used with caution – wherever you wish to make a bold statement. For instance, to flank a main door, space a pair of containers so that the distance between them is the same as the height of the door.

Use a single container to mark a focal point. A matching pair strategically placed will direct your eye towards it.

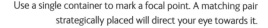

Working with Colour

Containers are often planted to bring colour to an area of paving or decking or an expanse of green lawn. Use colour judiciously to create a range of effects and moods – either vibrant and dynamic or calm and soothing.

Colour Theory and the Colour Wheel

There are three primary colours – red, blue and yellow – which cannot be created from other colours. The complementary colours of any of these primary colours – usually referred to as secondary colours – are a combination of the other two, as follows:

Primary	Complementary
Red	Green (Yellow + Blue)
Blue	Orange (Red + Yellow)
Yellow	Violet (Blue + Red)

The colour wheel organizes the colours in a way that illustrates the relationship between them. The primaries – red, yellow and blue – are arranged at three equally spaced points with the complementaries slotted in between them. Primaries therefore lie opposite their complementaries, as follows:

Red – Violet – Blue – Green – Yellow – Orange

Some containers combine more than one colour. The petals at the back of the flower, pointing upwards, are violet, while the lower ones are yellow and edged with violet – complementary colours.

The Colour Wheel

The colour wheel shows the relationships between different colours. As well as primary and secondary colours, there are also tertiary colours, which are created by mixing adjacent primary and secondary colours in various quantities.

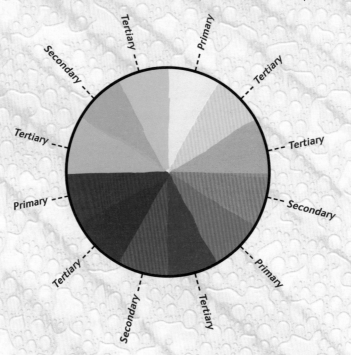

Colour Combinations

Artists and garden designers often use the colour wheel to inform their choice of colours. For instance, combining a primary colour with its complementary always creates a bold, exciting effect in a planting scheme – the complementary makes the primary pulsate and even shimmer (see the chart on page 98). For less of an impact, use a paler version of the primary – try pink with green; pale blue with orange; and cream with violet.

For maximum impact, use complementaries together. Colour schemes that use all the primary colours together generally look too 'busy' – the eye finds no resting place. For a more restful scheme, choose colours that are adjacent to each other (these are known as harmonizing colours) – perhaps adding paler tones of some of them. For instance, you might like to combine plant colours such as red, pink, lilac and violet and yellow, cream and orange.

Hot and Fiery

For a vibrant look, choose reds, yellows and oranges, perhaps with a dot of deep purple. Avoid pale colours entirely.

Cool and Sophisticated

For a cooler look, combine blues and/or purples with cream and white. You can also use grey and 'black' plants (see page 97).

Note: While colour theory should guide your choice of flowers, remember that in any planting it is virtually impossible to eliminate the colour green. Additionally, many flowers combine more than one colour – flowers may be mainly one colour but streaked with pink or red or have yellow centres.

Staying Neutral

If colour isn't your thing, or you simply do not want colour to dominate, there are plenty of plants in a range of subtle hues. Many grasses have beige or silvery brown flowers. Several plants have grey or silver leaves. Plants with grey leaves include:

Stachys lanata (bunnies' ears)

- *Ballota*
- *Convolvulus cneorum*
- *Helichrysum petiolare*
- *Hosta* (some)
- *Lavandula* (lavender)
- *Lotus berthelottii*
- *Salvia officinalis* (sage)
- *Stachys lanata* (bunnies' ears)

Soothing Green

Green is the most soothing to the eye of all the colours. Many interesting plantings might involve no flowers at all. Plantings of leafy hostas and bamboos can create a subtle but lush, almost tropical feel, particularly in a shady area.

Salvia officinalis (sage)

'Black' Plants

While there are many white plants, there are not so many black ones. The following have black (actually a very dark reddish purple in most cases) leaves, flowers or stems. These are often popular with designers who wish to create a dramatic look.

Aeonium 'Zwartkop'
Calla 'Blackjack'
Heuchera 'Plum Pudding'
Lathyrus odoratus 'Black Knight'
Ophiopogon planiscapus 'Nigrescens'
Phyllostachys nigra (black bamboo)
Scabiosa 'Ace of Spades'
Tulipa 'Queen of Night'
Viola 'Bowles' Black'

Black tulips

Top Tip

If you are using complementary colours, avoid adding white – it competes with the other two, effectively 'killing' them. The overall effect can be disappointing.

White petunias

Whiter Shade of Pale?

Many gardeners believe that white or very pale plantings are soothing and restful. This is not necessarily the case. White is the most dominant of all the colours and white objects often appear to 'loom' – because white reflects light, they appear bigger than they actually are. White and other pale colours come into their own in a predominantly shady area and at dusk as the light is beginning to fade.

Suggested Plant Combinations

The following is a suggestion for plants that combine well in containers, putting the principles of the colour wheel into practice.

Complementary schemes (for a bold effect)

Winter

Red	←——————→	Green
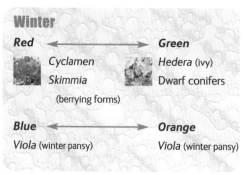

Red ←——————→ Green

Cyclamen — Hedera (ivy)

Skimmia — Dwarf conifers

(berrying forms)

Blue ←——————→ **Orange**

Viola (winter pansy) — Viola (winter pansy)

Spring

Red ←——————→ **Green**

Tulipa (tulip) — Hedera (Ivies)

Yellow ←——————→ **Violet**

Narcissus (daffodil) — Viola

Crocus — Hyacinthus

Tulipa (tulip) — (Hyacinth)

Blue ←——————→ **Orange**

Hyacinthus — Primula

(hyacinth)

Myosotis (forget-me-not) — Tulipa (tulip)

Summer

Red ←——————→ **Green**

Tropaeolum majus — Hosta

(nasturtium) — Hedera

Crocosmia 'Lucifer' — (ivy)

Ferns

Dahlia

Petunia

Zinnia

Yellow ←——————→ **Violet**

Calceolaria — Verbena

Helianthus (sunflower) — Viola

Blue ←——————→ **Orange**

Viola (pansy) — Viola (pansy)

Ageratum — Tropaeolum

(nasturtium)

Lobelia — Begonia

Harmonizing Schemes (for a soothing effect)

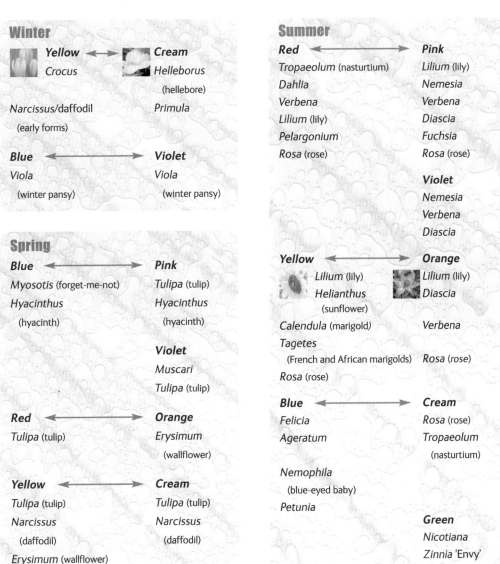

Winter

Yellow ← →	**Cream**
Crocus	Helleborus
	(hellebore)
Narcissus/daffodil	Primula
(early forms)	

Blue ← →	**Violet**
Viola	Viola
(winter pansy)	(winter pansy)

Spring

Blue ← →	**Pink**
Myosotis (forget-me-not)	Tulipa (tulip)
Hyacinthus	Hyacinthus
(hyacinth)	(hyacinth)
	Violet
	Muscari
	Tulipa (tulip)

Red ← →	**Orange**
Tulipa (tulip)	Erysimum
	(wallflower)

Yellow ← →	**Cream**
Tulipa (tulip)	Tulipa (tulip)
Narcissus	Narcissus
(daffodil)	(daffodil)
Erysimum (wallflower)	

Summer

Red ← →	**Pink**
Tropaeolum (nasturtium)	Lilium (lily)
Dahlia	Nemesia
Verbena	Verbena
Lilium (lily)	Diascia
Pelargonium	Fuchsia
Rosa (rose)	Rosa (rose)
	Violet
	Nemesia
	Verbena
	Diascia

Yellow ← →	**Orange**
Lilium (lily)	Lilium (lily)
Helianthus	Diascia
(sunflower)	
Calendula (marigold)	Verbena
Tagetes	
(French and African marigolds)	Rosa (rose)
Rosa (rose)	

Blue ← →	**Cream**
Felicia	Rosa (rose)
Ageratum	Tropaeolum
	(nasturtium)
Nemophila	
(blue-eyed baby)	
Petunia	
	Green
	Nicotiana
	Zinnia 'Envy'

Scented Schemes

While we often choose flowers on the basis of their colour, many are also deliciously scented. If you position your containers on a patio near open doors and windows, you can enjoy the scent without even setting foot outdoors.

Flower Scents

Flowers release their scent at different times of day, depending on when particular pollinating insects are active. Several waft out their scent in the early evening to attract moths. If you are out for most of the day, try positioning a pot of tobacco plants (*Nicotiana*) or – aptly named – night-scented stock (*Matthiola bicornis*) next to the front door to greet you with a puff of delicious fragrance when you get home from work.

Nicotiana

Aromatic Foliage

Some plants have aromatic oils in their leaves, which are released on contact. You can position containers of these near garden seats, so you can idly brush your hand over them to release the scent. Plants with scented leaves include:

 Anthemis nobilis
 Citrus
 Helichrysum italicum
 Laurus nobilis (bay)

Sweet basil

✅ *Lavandula* (lavender)

✅ *Mentha* (mint)

✅ *Ocimum basilicum* (sweet basil)

✅ *Pelargonium* (scented-leaf varieties)

✅ *Rosmarinus* (rosemary)

✅ *Ruta graveolens* (rue)*

✅ *Salvia officinalis* (sage)

✅ *Skimmia japonica*

* **Note**: People with sensitive skin sometimes develop a rash on contact with this plant, so it should be used with caution.

Plants with Scented Flowers

Winter/spring

Daphne

Narcissus/daffodil (early-flowering)

Rhododendron (some)

Sarcococca

Skimmia

Spring

Hyacinthus (hyacinth)

Narcissus/daffodil (some)

Paeonia (peony)

Rhododendron (some)

Syringa (lilac)

Syringa vulgaris (lilac)

Summer

Jasminum (jasmine)

Lathyrus odoratus (sweet pea)

Lilium/Lily (some)

Lonicera (honeysuckle)

Matthiola (stock)

Nicotiana (tobacco plant)

Petunia (dark blue varieties)

Rosa/rose (some)

Trachelospermum

Sarcococca humilis

Mint

Mint (*Mentha*) is normally a rampant plant, so many gardeners actually prefer to keep it in a pot to restrict its spread. Unlike most other herbs, it is also tolerant of shade, so does not need a prime position. Mint has a high water requirement, and the compost should never be allowed to dry out.

Along with traditional peppermint and spearmint types, there are many other varieties that have beguiling scents – sometimes quite unexpected. They include banana, ginger, pineapple, eau de cologne, basil, chocolate, lemon, lime and apple. For the strongest mint flavour, 'Tashkent' is often considered the best. For a refreshing after-dinner drink, pick a few leaves and lightly crush them with a pestle and mortar. Pour over boiling water, allow to stand for a few minutes, and then strain and serve.

Note: Lemon balm (*Melissa officinalis*), with lemon-scented leaves, can be used for a herb tea in the same way.

Get Cooking

Many aromatic plants are also edible. If you enjoy a summer barbecue, it is useful to have pots of these plants within picking distance. A few stems of rosemary flung over the coals will give off a fragrant smoke that gives a subtle Mediterranean flavour to any fish or meat on the barbecue.

Did You Know?

If you have a bay tree (Laurus nobilis) in a pot, and also have an open fire, you can cut off a few branches and toss them on to the flames. They burn with a crackle – doubly comforting on a cold winter evening.

Topiary in a Pot

Topiary – the art of clipping plants to shape – appeals to many gardeners. Many of the plants suitable for topiary are also suitable for growing in containers, as the frequent trimming keeps them well within bounds. Though you can buy ready-trimmed plants – usually balls or standards – it is very rewarding to create your own.

Plants for Shaping

Simple shapes are easiest for a beginner to tackle – a ball or dome is surprisingly easy to cut by eye. The following plants are very tolerant of regular clipping:

 Buxus (box)
 *Lavandula* (lavender)
 *Ligustrum* (privet)
 *Lonicera nitida*
 Taxus (yew)

Making a Start

The first spring after planting, shorten all the plant's stems to encourage bushy growth and a neat habit and then clip the plant to your desired shape.

Cube

Make an armature in the container. Drive four straight canes into the compost to mark the corners of the cube. Use horizontal canes to attach them at the top, tying them in position with wire or twine. Stretch chicken wire between the uprights and across the top to create the sides. Cut back any stems that grow beyond the armature. Once the shape is established, remove the armature and clip over three or four times a year as described for the ball or dome.

These box plants have been clipped into cubes that mirror the shapes of the containers they are planted in, creating further straight lines.

Ball or Dome

In summer, clip over all the new growth. Cut any long straggly shoots hard back, to the base if necessary (this will encourage vigorous new growth). Clip over again in late summer. The following year, cut to the desired shape in spring. Clip over again three or four times (but no later than late summer) to maintain a firm, even surface.

A Spiral of Gold

Cupressus macrocarpa 'Goldcrest' is a bright yellow conifer that is often sold as a hedging plant. Plants are naturally upright growing, in a teardrop shape, and it is easy to cut one into a spiral. Attach a brightly coloured cord to the tip of the plant with a clothes peg. Wrap the cord around the plant in a spiral, attaching it to the pot with masking tape. Using the cord as a guide, cut back the growth to the main stem. Once cut, the form is simple to maintain. Clip over three or four times a year to neaten.

Do try this at home – a spiral is easier to cut than you might think.

Cheat's Topiary

If you want a quick and easy topiary solution, use small-leaved ivies to cover a framework.
To make a simple obelisk, position four or five canes or bamboos around the perimeter of a large
container (*see* page 72). Plant an ivy at the base of each and tie in the flexible stems, training
them up the supports as they grow. For extra coverage, wrap chicken wire around the uprights or
run a separate wire up the frame in a spiral. Tie in all suitably placed shoots.

For more advanced shapes, make an armature with chicken wire. You can also buy ready-made
frames, often in more elaborate shapes – such as hearts, squirrels and teddy bears.

For a quick topiary effect, train small-leaved ivies onto supports – a tripod of canes makes a simple obelisk. Guide the
trailing stems upwards and attach them with wire ties.

A Water Garden in a Pot

It is quite possible to make a miniature water garden in a container. While small water features are available at garden centres, they are usually not designed to accommodate plants.

Planting Techniques

While a garden pond usually has a layer of mud at the bottom, for your mini pond, all the plants are best grown in individual containers or, preferably, aquatic baskets. Here are a few hints for success:

 Size: Choose the largest, deepest container you have room for – the larger the volume of water, the easier it is to keep it clear.

Most water plants are very rampant, but some, such as the miniature water lily on the left, are suitable for growing in smaller containers or even shallow pans.

☑ **Durability**: Besides being waterproof, the container must be durable. A plastic water tank – readily available at builders' merchants – is ideal.

☑ **Position**: Put the container in its final position before you fill with water – once filled, it will be very difficult to move.

☑ **Electricity**: If you want to incorporate a fountain, position the container near an outdoor power socket (which must be fitted by a qualified electrician), so that the electric cable does not trail across the ground.

☑ **Water level**: Top up the water regularly, both to maintain the level and to help keep the water clear.

☑ **Sun**: For optimum plant growth, the pond should be in full sun for most of the day.

Aquatic Baskets

Instead of using conventional plastic containers for the plants, use special ones designed for water plants. These are made from a plastic mesh that allows the water to pass freely through the sides. Use a large square container for a water lily, smaller ones for marginals.

Top Tip

If the container you're using is not a thing of beauty – for instance, if it is a black plastic water tank – disguise it with other plants in containers placed around the sides. These will also screen the pool from the sun in summer – which will heat the water and can lead to algal growth.

Compost

Conventional composts are unsuitable for aquatic plants. Use a special aquatic compost, which is made from a blend of sterilized loam, grit and dense peat. This has a low nutrient level to aid good plant growth without excessive nitrate release.

No Need to Feed

Feeding aquatic plants is unnecessary. With a permanent supply of water, all the plants grow vigorously, and there will be enough decayed plant matter dissolved in the water to meet their requirements.

Water Plants for Containers

Although there is a narrower choice of plants for growing in a water container garden, you can still create the effect of a lush-looking pond by selecting a mixture of water lilies (*Nymphaea*), marginal plants and oxygenating plants.

Water Lilies

With their spectacular flowers, water lilies are the most desirable of all water plants. Most varieties are much too vigorous for small ponds, but fortunately there are some miniatures that are ideal.

Water Lilies for a Mini Pool

'Aurora' (yellow, turning orange-red)

'Helvola' (yellow)

'Hermine' (white)

'Perry's Baby Red' (red)

'Shady Lady' (pink)

'Walter Pagels' (cream)

Water lilies have perfectly formed flowers that sit above the floating leaves. In a miniature pool, they repay a closer look.

Water hyacinth

Marginal Plants

Marginal water plants are plants that like to have water permanently around their roots. It is usual to grow these in containers even in a larger pool, as most can be invasive and this is a good way to restrict their spread. The compost should be slightly above or just level with the water. To achieve the correct depth, put piles of bricks in the container and set the marginals, planted in their baskets, on top.

Oxygenating Plants

There are a couple of plants that have a special application in water gardening. These are not planted in the conventional way, but just float under the surface of the water.

They are not decorative in their own right (though not ugly) – their function is to oxygenate the water, helping to keep it clear. Here are some useful plants for oxygentating the water:

- *Callitriche verna*
- *Fontinalis antipyretica* (**water moss**)
- *Lagarosiphon major*
- *Ranunculus aquatilis* (**water crowfoot**)

Ranunculus aquatilis (water crowfoot)

Keeping the Water Clear

Most pools are self-regulating, but during warm weather the water heats up and some evaporates. This can lead to excess algal growth (which you'll see as a green film on the water surface and around the sides of the container). You can deal with this with an algicide (choose one that is not toxic to plants – some are strictly for use in swimming pools and hot tubs), but you can reduce the risk of it taking over by regularly topping up the water each evening in summer. Not only does this maintain the correct water level, but it also helps cool the water. When you add fresh water, allow it to splash over the surface. This oxygenates the water, further discouraging algal growth.

Winter Care

Water in a container is much more likely to freeze in winter than water that's at ground level in a garden pond. And since water expands as it freezes, there's even the possibility that the ice will split the container. Wrap an old blanket around the container on the coldest nights – you can leave this on if the temperature remains below freezing during the daytime.

Keeping Fish

If you have fish in the pond – which are less active in winter – make a hole in any surface ice by holding a saucepan filled with boiling water over it until a hole has melted. Do not be tempted to break the ice, as the shock waves can kill fish.

Style Gallery

The following section illustrates some possible plant and container combinations to achieve a particular look.

Pots and Planters

A Summer's Day

Type of container: Weathered wooden half barrel
Plant choice: A clean-looking blend of creamy yellow arctotis with an underplanting of blue and white lobelia. This seasonal display, using annual plants, has been planted for summer interest.
Ideal position: A sunny position on a deck, near wooden panel fencing or anywhere in a cottage garden would suit this informal scheme.
Note: This barrel has not been treated with a preservative, so must be lined with thick plastic before planting.

Year-round Interest

Type of container: Shallow pan raised above ground level
Plant choice: A range of slow-growing succulents, including echeveriums, sedums and agaves, which will be of interest throughout the year. White marble chippings set off the planting. This display will look good over a number of years.
Ideal position: Full sun, ideally near paving or brickwork/stonework that will reflect light and heat back on to the plants.
Note: These plants are best if given some shelter from heavy rainfall.

Cottage Delight

Type of container: Wooden barrel

Plant choice: White trailing bacopa and orange chrysanthemums make a simple combination for summer interest. Although these plants are perennial, they often exhaust themselves, so are best discarded after flowering.

Ideal position: Full sun or lightly shaded, in a cottage garden or as part of an informal scheme.

Note: Because of the bulbous shape of the container, it may be practical to plant up a plastic container and then sink this into the barrel.

Colour Therapy

Type of container: Decorative pottery urn

Plant choice: Blue lobelia, white bacopa and pink petunias, planted for summer interest. This soothing combination has been devised so as not to detract from the interest of the container.

Ideal position: Sun or light shade, on a patio or deck.

Note: As these plants are not deep-rooted, they are best planted in a shallower plastic container that sits in the rim of the urn.

Bold Style

Type of container:
Geometric pottery container
Plant choice: Tropical red-flowered guzmania and ornamental trailing asparagus. These are perennial evergreen plants that can stay in the container for several years. This very simple combination takes its strength from the guzmania's firm outline.
Ideal position: Lightly shaded position on a deck or patio. This container is suitable for use indoors, in a bright situation but away from direct sunlight.
Note: These plants will not tolerate frost.

A Burst of Beauty

Type of container:
Large terracotta planter
Plant choice: A generous mix of summer-flowering plants, using predominantly harmonizing colours with felted grey foliage. A clever use has been made of proportion – the volume occupied by the planting is twice that of the container.
Ideal position: A sunny position on a terrace or patio, but sheltered from strong winds because of the height of the plants.

Simple Pleasures

Type of container:
Antique terracotta pot

Plant choice: Red impatiens with blue and white lobelias and trailing *Helichrysum petiolare*. A simple planting such as this will give pleasure over many weeks in summer. The flowering plants can be discarded after flowering, but it's possible to keep the helichrysum over winter if you take cuttings in late summer.

Ideal position: Best in light shade, on a deck or patio in a cottage or informal garden.

Form Over Colour

Type of container: Group of weathered terracotta containers

Plant choice: Scented-leaf pelargoniums, begonias and gazanias. These plants are being grown more for the interest of their leaves – the flowers seem almost incidental – as a contrast to the spiky phormiums in the border that makes a backdrop.

Ideal position: Full sun in a relaxed but contemporary setting, where the emphasis is as much on line and shape as it is on colour.

Sun Worshipper

Type of container: Decorative pottery

Plant choice: A rich combination of gazanias and arctotis, with purple-leaved *Lobelia cardinalis* (which will later produce scarlet flowers) for summer interest.

Ideal position: Full sun in a paved or gravel area.

Note: Like many other daisy plants, gazanias open their flowers only in full sun. They close during cloudy conditions. The lobelia is a perennial that can be planted out in the garden in autumn or potted up for use next year.

Sculptural Sophistication

Type of container: Rectangular burnished metal

Plant choice: A clipped box ball (a variegated form of *Buxus sempervirens*) and a yew obelisk (*Taxus baccata*) underplanted with black grass (*Ophiopogon planiscapus* 'Nigrescens'). This is a very understated, sculptural planting that relies for its effect on precise geometry and proportion.

Ideal position: Sun or shade on a roof garden, balcony or other contemporary space.

Note: The plants will need regular clipping to keep them looking smart.

Radiant Warmth

Type of container:

Decorative terracotta container

Plant choice: Orange gazanias and red cupheas. This rich but harmonizing combination has been devised to have impact without detracting from the charm of the container. The whole ensemble radiates warmth.

Ideal position: Full sun in a prominent position, so the container can be fully appreciated.

Note: The cuphea is actually a subshrub but does not tolerate frost. Plants can be overwintered provided they can be kept in frost-free conditions.

Mediterranean Appeal

Type of container:

Mediterranean terracotta urn

Plant choice: Creamy yellow Mexican marigold (*Tagetes lemmonii*), which has ferny grey foliage, makes a subtle – even unexpected – statement, with a touch of red to arrest the attention. This shrubby plant will flower throughout the summer.

Ideal position:

A sunny position in a Mediterranean or gravel garden.

Note: The leaves of this plant have a pungent aroma that is released on contact. The yellow flowers will attract hoverflies and other pollinating insects.

Window Boxes

Pelargoniums Shine

Type of container:
Moulded lightweight plastic
Plant choice: Red and pink pelargoniums –
upright and trailing forms – pale blue
lobelias and light purple petunias planted
tightly to make a summer display that will
last for many weeks. Restricting the colour
palette allows the red flowers to sing out
when they appear.
Ideal position: Full sun is needed for the
pelargoniums to flower best. If omitted, this
combination would tolerate some shade.

Quirky Style

Type of container: Hand-made painted
wooden box with integral bird box
Plant choice: Blue angelonia, blue lobelia
and white verbena make a surprisingly
sophisticated combination for summer –
an intriguing contrast to the weathered
rustic-looking container and the picket
fence behind.
Ideal position: This quirky box needs a
prominent position in full sun. The bird box is
purely decorative and unlikely to be used.
Note: A wooden box such as this should be
lined with black plastic before planting.

A Display for Winter

Type of container: Moulded plastic

Plant choice: Spotted laurel
(*Aucuba japonica* 'Crotonifolia'),
dwarf skimmias (*Skimmia japonica*
'Rubella') and purple-leaved heuchera
with trailing ivies for a winter display
that will be effective for several
months. The rich pink buds of the
skimmias will open to scented white
flowers in late winter.

Ideal position: These are tough
plants that will do well in almost any
situation apart from deep shade.

Note: The plants can be potted up or
planted out in the garden in spring.

Transitional Tactics

Type of container: Two small plastic window
boxes, side by side

Plant choice: A riotous mix of dwarf red tulips,
late small-cupped daffodils and blue, yellow and
orange winter pansies. The pansies will be in
flower from late winter onwards and the bulbs will
rise above them to flower from mid to late spring.

Ideal position: A sunny position sheltered from
strong winds.

Note: Several small boxes placed adjacent to
each other can give the impression of a single
long container.

Simplicity Wins

Type of container:
White painted window box

Plant choice: A simple combination of bright red pelargoniums and trailing variegated glechoma. Less can often be more, as this window box amply demonstrates – the simple, even obvious, planting combination, majoring on the complementaries of red and green, makes the strongest possible impact against the white house.

Ideal position: For optimum flowering, the box should be facing full sun.

A Riot of Colour

Type of container:
Synthetic window box

Plant choice: Red pelargoniums and harmonizing yellow and orange marigolds (*Tagetes*) and California poppies (*Eschscholzia*) – all of which have a guaranteed long flowering period in summer.

Ideal position: Full sun, with protection from strong winds.

Note: Boxes positioned on a balustrade or rail must be very firmly attached. It can be simpler to suspend them on brackets that fit over the rail.

An Exercise in Symmetry

Type of container:

Moulded synthetic container

Plant choice: Pale blue lobelia and contrasting yellow pansies flanking a blue hydrangea in the centre. The symmetrical summer scheme implies formality, reflecting the strict geometry of the window frame and shutters.

Ideal position: A position in partial shade is best, so the hydrangea flowers will hold their colour.

Note: If the hydrangea is in an individual container, it can be lifted and replaced when the flowers fade – the other plants will probably keep going for longer.

Hanging Baskets

A Cone of Colour

Type of container: Small, conical wicker basket

Plant choice: Lilac and cream petunias, blue lobelias and orange verbenas for summer. The plants are colourful, but compact and upright-growing. Usually, trailing plants are used in a basket, but in this case they would detract from its charm and spoil the line.

Ideal position: A sheltered spot in sun or dappled shade.

Note: Wicker must be lined with plastic – most similar baskets are sold ready-lined.

Trailing Tradition

Type of container: Traditional plastic-coated wire basket with liner

Plant choice: Flamboyant, bi-coloured, frilly-edged petunias and miniature red begonias. This is a typical – but no less effective for that – hanging basket planting with showy trailing summer annuals that will in time conceal the basket and its liner.

Ideal position: A partially shaded spot is best, with some shelter from strong winds.

A Harmony of Hues

Type of container:
Traditional basket
Plant choice: Harmonizing pink
and red trailing pelargoniums that
will be in flower throughout the
summer. With regular feeding and
watering, these plants will rapidly
grow to form a ball of flowers that
seems to float in the air. Using
multiples of a single plant is bold
but generally extremely effective.
Ideal position: Full sun,
but with protection from
strong winds.

Bold Contrasts

Type of container:
Traditional basket
Plant choice: A generous mix of
white, pink and blue petunias. The
flamboyant use of the same plant in
different colours makes the strongest
possible impact next to the front door.
Ideal position: A position with some
shade from strong sun would
be best and prolong the life of the
individual flowers.
Note: For a more harmonious look,
omit the white flowers.

checklist

- **Container choice:** Choose containers to achieve the look you want. Match the plants to the container. Similar containers in a range of sizes create an integrated look.

- **Formal v. informal:** For formality, use even numbers of containers in a strictly symmetrical arrangement. Odd numbers work best if you are aiming at a more casual look.

- **Placement:** The golden section or Fibonacci numbers can help in placing containers in a pleasing arrangement, although you should still trust your own instinct.

- **Colour effects:** Use colour to provide bold splashes or more subtle effects. Referring to the colour wheel can help you make choices, or just experiment with plants in flower.

- **Unusual colours:** 'Black' plants always have a strong presence, especially in a very modernist, minimalist scheme.

- **Soothing green:** Plenty of greenery – from leaves, bamboos and grasses – will have a soothing, tranquil effect.

- **Using white:** Be careful how you use white – it can be a very strong colour.

- **Scent:** Add to the sensuous appeal of the planting with scented plants. Some plants have scented leaves as well as flowers.

- **Water:** Bring water into a paved area by creating a pond in a large container. Plant with a miniature water lily and marginal water plants in pots.

Container Gardening Through The Year

Spring

Spring is a time when most of us want to see fresh colour – especially if the winter has been a long and hard one. This is a time to major on early bulbs, which often have rich saturated colours.

Instant Colour

For an instant effect with minimum effort, visit a garden centre or nursery and buy plants in flower. Try mixing and matching different plants before you buy to be sure you end up with a pleasing combination.

Note: When shopping for plants in flower, don't forget to add a few 'fillers' such as trailing ivies or dwarf conifers. These can be a good investment, as they can be used in other plantings throughout the rest of the year.

Plants for Spring Interest

Shrubs and Climbers

Camellia

Clematis alpina

Clematis macropetala

Rhododendron

Skimmia japonica

Bulbs

Anemone blanda

Crocus

Fritillaria meleagris
  (fritillary)

Hyacinthus (hyacinth)

Iris danfordiae

Iris reticulata

Muscari
  (grape hyacinth)

Narcissus (daffodil)

Scilla

Tulipa (tulip)

Perennials

Bergenia

Helleborus (hellebore)

Annuals

Bellis

Erysimum (wallflower)

Myosotis
  (forget-me-not)

Primula
  (polyanthus types)

Viola (pansy)

Viola (pansies)

Classic Spring Combinations

Some plants seem to have been made for each other and always make happy marriages. Pink tulips are often combined with blue forget-me-nots (*Myosotis*). Wallflowers (*Erysimum*) are available in a wide colour range – cream, yellow, orange and a rich dark red – that allows for any number of possible colour effects, harmonious, complementary or boldly clashing.

For a very sophisticated look, try using the same colour for the different plants – for instance, orange tulips underplanted with orange pansies or polyanthus (perhaps with yellow-variegated ivies to soften the container's edge).

Spring Hanging Baskets

While hanging baskets are normally planted for summer interest, some spring-flowering plants make ideal subjects. As the weather can still be cool, the plants will not grow much, so it is doubly important to cram them in for the best effect. (For details on how to plant a basket, *see* page 54.) After flowering, either discard the plants, pot them up or plant them in the garden. Some ideal plants for a spring basket include:

- *Crocus*
- *Hedera* (ivy)
- *Muscari* (grape hyacinth)
- *Narcissus* (daffodil; dwarf varieties)
- *Primula* (polyanthus types)
- *Viola*

Forward Planning with Bulbs

Large containers can be planted up in late autumn for flowers in spring. This is when most bulbs are sold loose, which is a much more economic way of acquiring them than as plants in flower later on. You'll also have a much wider choice of varieties. For a wider choice still, consult a bulb catalogue or order online for autumn delivery – much the best way of obtaining unusual varieties and newer ones, of which there may be limited stock.

Planting Bulbs

Ignore the recommended spacings for bulb planting in the garden. Containers are planted for maximum impact, so plant in layers, as many as the container will hold, as described below.

While a single variety will make a strong statement, you can also mix varieties for various colour effects (*see* page 98). For a very sophisticated look, try using black and white tulips (e.g. 'Queen of the Night' and 'Maureen') – but be sure to choose varieties that flower at the same time.

 Drainage: Line the base of a large container with stones or crocks so that the drainage holes are covered (but not blocked).

Top Tip

When buying bulbs to use in a mixed display, carefully check the eventual height of the plant, flower size and flowering time (these will all be indicated on the packaging).

Compost: Put in a layer of compost (preferably mixed with grit, sand or perlite or vermiculite for improved drainage).

First layer: Set a number of bulbs in a ring on the compost surface. They should not touch each other or be in contact with the inner side of the container. Sprinkle in more compost to come halfway up the bulbs.

Second layer: Put in a second layer of bulbs to sit in the spaces between the bulbs below (making sure they do not touch). Add more compost, filling to about 2 cm (1 in) below the rim of the container to allow for watering.

Note: Depending on the diameter of the container, there may be room for two further rings of bulbs within the outer two.

Planting Depths for Bulbs

Bulbs are normally planted approximately to twice their own depth. In other words, if a bulb measures 5 cm (2 in) from base to tip, it should have a 10 cm (4 in) depth of compost above it. Large containers are best, therefore, as you also need to allow for enough compost underneath each bulb for good root growth.

Bulbs for Successional Interest

Stunning though a single variety may be, you can prolong the interest of the container by choosing two different bulb varieties to flower in succession. Plant them in layers, as described. The advantage of this method is that the later-flowering bulbs will conceal the foliage of the early ones as they die back. It's best if the flowering periods are several weeks apart, so that the late bulbs are not sufficiently advanced to then crowd out the early ones when they are in flower. Suitable bulb combinations include:

 Early irises with late daffodils, hyacinths or tulips

 Early crocuses with late daffodils, hyacinths or tulips

Early dwarf daffodils with late tulips or hyacinths

Did You Know?

A bulb already contains the flower within it – hence no additional feeding is necessary until after the bulb has flowered (when it will have expended all its energy).

Top Tip

After planting a container with bulbs, sprinkle some grass seed on the compost surface. This will germinate rapidly, so the bulbs will rise up through a mini lawn.

Caring for Bulbs in Containers

After planting, water the container periodically over winter so that the compost never dries out (the bulbs are already growing beneath the compost surface). Once they appear above ground level in late winter to early spring, water them frequently (though they do not need feeding). After flowering, empty out the container and discard the bulbs. Wash the container well before using it for a summer display. (Before emptying a container, allow the compost to dry out first.)

Keeping Bulbs

If you want to keep the bulbs after flowering, remove the faded flower heads. Feed the bulbs with a general garden fertilizer. When the foliage starts to turn yellow, stop watering and feeding (unless there are other plants in the container that need this). Once the bulbs have died back, empty the container and excavate the bulbs. Brush off any crumbs of compost clinging to the bulbs. Leave them in the sun (or in a warm dry place such as a kitchen) to dry off completely. Once dry, store the bulbs in paper bags in a cold but dry place (such as a garage or shed). Replant them the following autumn.

Note: Only firm healthy bulbs should be stored. Discard any soft and/or damaged ones.

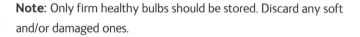

Summer

This is the season when most of us want to spend the maximum amount of time outdoors, enjoying the garden. Even if you have only a courtyard, deck, roof terrace or balcony, it can still be full of colour – a place of retreat for enjoying sunny days and balmy evenings.

Bedding Plants

These are plants that are sold in modules in garden centres and nurseries from late spring onwards. They are nearly all ideal for use in containers and will flower throughout the summer. It's cheaper to raise your own plants from seed, however. For the best results, use F_1 hybrids, which always germinate easily (for more information, *see* page 190).

No other group of plants provides such a range of colour over such as long period as summer annuals. Whether you buy small plants or raise your own, a succession of flowers is guaranteed.

What is an Annual?

An annual is a plant that completes its lifecycle within a 12-month period. Usually, a seed germinates in spring to produce a plant that flowers in summer. Once pollinated, the flowers produce seed and the plant dies. The seed stays dormant until the following spring.

Sowing Annuals

If you want to have flowers until the first frosts, make two sowings. Sow in early to mid spring, so you'll have plants that will start flowering in early summer. Then make a second sowing in early summer that you can use to replace the first sowing – which will be exhausted by mid to late summer.

Compost: Fill modules or trays with a seed or multi-purpose compost. Water the compost thoroughly and then allow to drain.

Seed: Sow the seed on the compost surface, lightly pressing it down to ensure good adhesion.

Cover: Lightly cover the seed with compost sprinkled through your fingers or with sand or perlite or vermiculite. The seed must be covered.

Position: Put the seed in a light sheltered place (but out of direct sun) until it germinates.

Note: The second sowing can be made in containers outdoors.

Top Tip

Sow annual seed as finely as you can, handling the seeds individually as far as is possible. This means you will not need to thin the seedlings later.

Plants for Wildlife

Container gardening is not like ordinary gardening. In a large space, it's easy to have a few trees for birds to nest and perch in, with berries and nuts for them and small mammals to feed on in winter. Also, you can regularly replenish the soil with your own homemade compost and other organic matter to keep it teeming with invertebrate and microbial life. This is much more difficult with containers, where you are using proprietary composts (that contain no earthworms or other soil-dwelling organisms) and regularly applying artificial fertilizers to keep your plants healthy and flowering well.

Nevertheless, it's still possible to have an outdoor space humming with valuable insect life, especially in summer, even if you have no soil at all. The following plants are known to be attractive to bees and other pollinating insects:

- *Antirrhinum* (snapdragon)
- *Buddleja*
- *Clematis*
- *Fuchsia*
- *Lavandula* (lavender)
- *Limnanthes* (fried egg plant)
- *Rosmarinus* (rosemary)
- *Sedum acre* (stonecrop)
- *Tagetes* (French and African marigolds)
- *Verbena bonariensis*

Tagetes (marigold)

Roses

Roses are truly a plant of summer, producing quantities of gorgeous flowers throughout the season in a wide range of colours – white, cream, yellow, pink, orange and red. While many make large plants that need correspondingly large containers, there are a number of types that have been bred specifically to meet the needs of gardeners with limited space.

- **Patio roses**: Neat-growing plants – usually around 45 cm (18 in) high – that are well-clothed with glossy, usually disease-free foliage.

- **Miniature roses**: These are smaller than patio roses – generally within 30 cm (12 in) – and more twiggy.

- **Ground-cover roses**: Growing to 30 cm (12 in) high, these are similar in appearance to patio roses but have lax spreading stems.

- **Miniature climbers**: These also have longer stems than patio roses and are suitable for training against a wall or on a support set in the container. They usually achieve a height of around 1.5 m (5 ft).

Did You Know?

Unlike most garden roses, roses suitable for container cultivation need no complicated pruning regime. Simply clip or shear them over in early spring, then again in midsummer.

Caring for Roses

To get the best out of your roses, use a good-quality, soil-based compost (see page 44). You can still get good results from a soil-less mix, but will need t0 increase the feeding. Routine rose-care tasks include:

Watering the plants freely during spring and summer.

 Feeding well, using a rose or tomato fertilizer.

Removing flowers as they fade. This will encourage the plant to carry on producing flowers.

Tender Perennials

A valuable group of summer plants are the so-called tender perennials – plants that will not survive frost. They grow and flower throughout the summer and are all ideal for use in containers. After flowering (late summer to early autumn) you have a number of choices:

 Discard the plants.

 Take cuttings to grow on indoors and use next year.

Pot up the plants and keep them in a heated conservatory. (Many will carry on flowering during this period.)

Tender Plants that Flower Best in Full Sun

Osteospermum

Brachyscome

Diascia

Felicia (blue daisy)

Gazania

Helichrysum petiolare
   (grey or yellow felted foliage)

Lotus berthelottii (silver foliage)

Nemesia

Osteospermum

Pelargonium

Verbena

Fuchsias

Fuchsias are essential plants for summer containers. Most are compact or have trailing stems that make them ideal for hanging baskets, either on their own or as the main plant. You can also buy them trained as standards – useful for more formal displays, or just used to provide flowers at eye level, rising above smaller bedding plants or trailing ivies.

Flowers can be slim and dainty or big and blowsy – both have their uses. Triphylla types (which do not tolerate frost) have sumptuous velvety leaves, providing the perfect foil to their coral red or pink flowers.

Keeping Fuchsias

While many gardeners are content to discard their fuchsias at the end of the flowering season, it is worth keeping them for next year, especially if you have a favourite variety.

- **Sun:** In late summer, put the plant in the sunniest possible position. Exposure to heat will ripen the woody parts of the plant.

- **Fertilizer:** Feed well with a potassium-high fertilizer – a tomato or hanging basket feed is ideal. This also firms the wood.

- **Store:** When the leaves have shrivelled and fallen, and before the first frosts, put the plants in a cool but frost-free environment, such as an unheated greenhouse or porch (or unheated spare bedroom).

- **Water:** Over winter, water the plants sparingly, just to prevent the compost from drying out.

- **Cut back:** The following spring, cut the plants back, start watering more frequently and begin feeding. This will build up the plants for flowering in the summer.

Autumn

This can be a busy time in the garden, as you will be emptying out summer containers that have now finished. While you may already be planning next year's containers over the coming months, there is still much to enjoy.

Flowers for Autumn

If you made a late sowing of annuals (*see* page 133), these will still be going strong. Provided they have been well watered, fed and dead-headed, fuchsias, pelargoniums and other tender perennials (*see* page 136) will also be flowering well. Many roses put on an excellent display at this time of year, sometimes better than the summer one. Cooler temperatures seem to suit them and flowers will often last longer.

Pelargonium

Berries

Berries are ripening at this time of year. Skimmias will berry reliably even as very small plants, and, with their neat habit, they make ideal container plants. Gaultherias (which do best in ericaceous compost) are small plants with large berries that can be white, pink, red or purple.

Note: Birds tend not to strip berries from plants in containers, as they are usually kept so close to the house.

Taking Cuttings

This is a good time of year for taking cuttings, especially from tender perennials (see page 136) and fuchsias. Although you can pot these up for use next year (provided you can overwinter them in frost-free conditions), the plants may have become woody at the base, with a mass of straggly leafless stems. Cuttings will give you plenty of new plants for next summer.

Shoot: Cut strong shoots from the plant, about 5–7.5 cm (2–3 in) long.

Cut: Trim each cutting at the base just below the lowest set of leaves. Trim off the leaves from the lower half of the cutting.

Compost: Insert the cuttings in pots or trays filled with moistened multi-purpose compost mixed with sharp sand. The lowest leaves should be just above the compost surface.

Cover: Tent the cuttings in a clear plastic bag.

Store: Keep the cuttings in a light place – such as on a windowsill – but out of direct sunlight. They should root within about six weeks. Pot the cuttings up, watering them sparingly in winter. Start feeding and watering more regularly in spring.

A Harem of Hollies

Hollies mostly have red berries (though there are a few with yellow). The plants are unusual in that male and female flowers are produced on different specimens. In order to ensure berries, you need a female form with a male nearby – one male will pollinate five or more females. 'J.C. van Tol.', however, can berry without a male in the vicinity.

Rooting Cuttings in Water

Tender perennials can also be rooted in water in a glass jar on a windowsill in the house (as long as they are not in direct sunlight). Take the cuttings as described, then suspend them over the water on cocktail sticks that support the lowest leaves and sit on the rim of the jar. The base of the cutting must trail in the water. Change the water regularly to prevent it turning green. Once the roots are well formed, pot up the cuttings in ordinary potting compost. Water them lightly over winter and then start feeding the following spring to develop good plants for the summer.

Note: Roots made in water tend to be very brittle. Handle them very carefully when potting up the cuttings to avoid breaking them.

Colour from Leaves

The foliage of several deciduous plants glows in rich shades of orange, yellow and red at this time of year, as green pigments break down before the leaves are shed or die back. On some evergreens – such as bergenias – cold weather causes the foliage to redden. Plants with good autumn leaf colour include:

Acer japonicum (Japanese maple)

 Acer japonicum   ***Paeonia* (peony)**

 Acer palmatum ***Rhus typhina***

Bergenia ***'Dissecta'***

Hosta ***Trachelospermum***

Sowing Sweet Peas

While spring is the usual time for sowing annuals, you will get a better performance from sweet peas (*Lathyrus odoratus*) if you sow them in autumn. This allows them to develop deep roots that will produce vigorous growth – and earlier flowers – next year.

Compost: Fill 12.5 cm (5 in) pots with seed or multi-purpose compost (ideally with added sharp sand). Water the pots and allow to drain.

Seed: Make small holes in the compost with a dibber, then put a seed in each hole. Sow 5–7 seeds per pot, evenly spaced. Draw the surrounding compost over each seed to cover.

Position: Put the pots in a sheltered spot outdoors. The seed will germinate rapidly. The seedlings must be kept cool over the coming months (for the best root development). Keep them in a cold frame that will protect them from the worst of the weather, as well as from slugs and mice.

Repot: In early spring, knock the seedlings out from the container and pot them up in a large container to grow on.

Note: Since sweet peas resent root disturbance, they should be sown and grown on in the same container until you are ready to pot them up in spring.

Camellias

If you grow camellias in containers, they need special attention during autumn, as this is the time of year when they are building their flowers for the spring display. You should already be able to see the buds developing. It's crucial to keep the plants well watered during this period. If allowed to dry out, the plant will shed the buds before they open.

Winter

The winter months can be gloomy, but there's no need to be without colour – or scent – from your containers.

Winter-flowering shrubs

A number of shrubs flower in winter. Winter jasmine (*Jasminum nudiflorum*) can be spectacular in a large container – the arching stems are covered in bright yellow flowers. The evergreen *Viburnum tinus* also flowers at this time of year, with clusters of white flowers that look like little posies. The flowers of Christmas box (*Sarcococca*) are not showy, but are sweetly scented. Comparably fragrant are winter-flowering daphnes. Place pots of these near the front door to be sure to enjoy the scent on a regular basis.

Bellis perennis

Viburnum tinus

Plants for Colour

Some plants flower in winter – or, more accurately, intermittently during mild spells. Heathers (*Erica*) are among the most reliable – there are also varieties with yellow, orange or bronze foliage. Winter pansies (*Viola*) produce flowers over a long period in a wide range of colours. Polyanthus primroses and *Bellis perennis* (with pink, white or red flowers) can be used for flowers at the end of winter.

Cyclamen (varieties of *Cyclamen persicum*) are often sold in winter for use in containers. They have white, pink or red flowers. While these can be very effective – especially in window boxes – the plants are not reliably hardy. In frost-prone areas, use them for containers in a sheltered position or be prepared to replace them if any succumb to the cold.

Hellebores

Hellebores (*Helleborus*) all do well in containers, either on their own or combined with other plants. The Christmas rose (*Helleborus niger*) produces its glistening white flowers in the very depths of winter. Most other hellebores flower slightly later, but well before spring. Flower colours include white, pink, apple green, creamy yellow, cherry red and a bold slate purple. The flowers can be dramatically streaked or spotted with maroon. Some very desirable forms have double flowers. For container use, it's best to buy small compact plants in flower.

Hellebore leaves are also eye-catching, in many cases being marbled with silver or white. Later in the year, they make effective companions to other flowering plants.

Year-round Interest

Several plants make a contribution year-round – though it is often in autumn and winter, when there are inevitably fewer flowers, that we value them most. At these quiet times of year, their shapes and subtle colours come into their own.

Underplanting

If you take a minimalist approach to design, you will appreciate the lines and shapes made by evergreen plants without any further adornment. However, it's perfectly possible to add interest and colour by planting round the edge of the container. This planting need not be permanent – though it can be – so you can ring in the changes even while the central plant stays the same. Add small bulbs in autumn by making small holes in the compost, pressing in the bulb and then topping with the excavated compost.

Permanent Plants

Small plants that can provide interest from one year to the next include small-leaved ivies (*Hedera helix*), with either plain green leaves or leaves marked and margined with yellow, cream, white or silver, and the black grass (*Ophiopogon planiscapus* 'Nigrescens').

Top Tip

The perfect tool for underplanting is a narrow trowel, which will minimize possible damage to the main plant's root system.

Plants for Year-round Interest

Buxus (box)

Euonymus

Hebe

Hedera (ivy)

Ilex (holly)

Laurus nobilis (bay)

Ligustrum (privet)

Phoenix canariensis
(date palm)

Phormium

Skimmia

Taxus (yew)

Trachycarpus fortunei

Bulbs

Small early bulbs generally work best. Though it's possible to underplant with dwarf tulips and narcissi, these will look untidy as they die back. There are many varieties of crocus in shades of white, cream, lilac and purple. Grape hyacinth (*Muscari*) flowers are slate purple. Equally subtle are snake's-head fritillaries (*Fritillaria melegaris*). The ordinary one has nodding flowers that are also chequered with grey-purple, but there is also a very subtle form with cream flowers for an elegant understated effect.

Seasonal Plants

For winter interest, choose from reliable winter pansies (*Viola*), with cream, yellow, orange, maroon or blue flowers (some blotched with darker colours), or, for late winter to early spring, polyanthus primulas. These have jewel-like flowers in white, cream, pink, yellow, red and purple.

Muscari
(grape hyacinth)

For summer, use small bedding plants that stay compact. Good choices include lobelias (in red, blue or white), ageratums (shades of blue) and French and African marigolds (*Tagetes*), with yellow or orange flowers.

Ageratums

Container Plants Directory

Unless otherwise indicated, plants in the following directory will withstand temperatures down to –10°C (14°F). 'H' stands for height, 'S' stands for spread.

Trees, shrubs and Climbers

Acer japonicum, A. palmatum
Japanese maple
Elegant deciduous trees grown for their foliage, which usually turns rich red, orange and yellow before falling in autumn. They need shade and a very sheltered position.
H 1.1 m (4 ft), S 1.1 m (4 ft)

Agave americana
Century plant
An architectural succulent with fleshy, pointed leaves. Use it on its own in a large container or as an impressive centrepiece to a summer planting. It needs winter protection in frost-prone areas.
H 1 m (3 ft), S 1 m (3 ft)

Agave americana
(century plant)

Aucuba japonica 'Crotonifolia'
Spotted laurel
A much-maligned evergreen shrub that looks sensational in a container, with large leathery, glossy leaves that are generously marked with yellow. It thrives in shade. Prune often to maintain a compact neat habit.
H 1 m (3 ft), S 1 m (3 ft)

Berberis
Thorny evergreen or deciduous shrubs with yellow or orange spring flowers and autumn berries. Some have beautifully marked leaves. They can be clipped to keep them in bounds (though this can affect flowering and fruiting).
H 1.5 m (5 ft), S 1 m (3 ft), more or less, depending on the variety

Buxus sempervirens
Box
Evergreen shrubs that can be clipped to maintain a firm outline. They are ideal for small topiary and are often sold trained as

standards. They thrive in sun or shade.
H 1 m (3 ft), S 1 m (3 ft) but can be kept
much smaller with regular trimming.

Calluna
Heather

There are many varieties of *Calluna*, mostly
summer-flowering, with white, pink, red or
purple flowers (some with coloured foliage).
They are good bee plants. Trim back after
flowering. **Note:** Heathers must be grown
in ericaceous compost. For winter heathers,
see *Erica*.
H 30 cm (12 in), S 20 cm (8 in)

Camellia

Camellia
Glamorous evergreen shrubs with white, pink
or red flowers in spring (some types can
flower in autumn and winter). Potentially
large plants, they can be kept neat by pruning
after flowering. **Note:** Camellias must be
grown in ericaceous compost.
H 2 m (6 ft), S 1 m (3 ft)

Citrus (orange tree)

Citrus
Elegant evergreen trees and shrubs that in
favourable areas will produce edible fruits
(oranges, lemons and limes). They will not
withstand frost, so may need winter
protection. Clip over regularly to keep
them neat.
H 2 m (6 ft), S 1 m (3 ft)

Clematis
Many of these climbers are too vigorous for
containers, but some have been bred for the
purpose. Most produce their flowers – mainly
white, pink, blue and purple – in summer.
They die back in winter.
H 2 m (6 ft) more or less, depending on the
variety, S 60 cm (2 ft).

Convolvulus cneorum
Neat-growing evergreen shrubs with beautiful
downy, silver leaves and a succession of white
funnel-shaped flowers
in summer. It must have gritty compost.
H 60 cm (24 in), S 90 cm (36 in)

Cordyline

Cordyline

Evergreen palms with a tropical or architectural look. They need winter protection in cold areas.
H 1.5 m (5 ft), S 60 cm (2 ft)

Cycas revoluta

Japanese sago palm

A thick-stemmed palm with long feathery leaves. It needs winter protection in frost-prone areas.
H 2 m (6 ft), S 1.1 m (4 ft)

Daphne

Deciduous or evergreen shrubs grown for their deliciously scented flowers (white, yellow, pink, lilac or purple), often in late winter. They resent pruning.
H 90 cm (36 in), S 60 cm (24 in), more or less, depending on the species.

Dicksonia antarctica

Australian tree fern

This tree fern has a tropical look, with large fronds that die back in cold winters. The trunk grows only 2.5 cm (1 in) per year, so buy an established specimen. Protect the top of the plant in cold winters.
H 1.2 m (5 ft) or more, S 1.1 m (4 ft)

Dracaena

These architectural palms, with strappy leaves, can be multi-stemmed trees or just shoot from the base. They are excellent on their own or underplanted with trailing plants. They need winter protection.
H 60 cm (24 in), S 60 cm (24 in); types that develop trunks can be much bigger.

Dracaena

Erica
Heather

There are many types of *Erica*, with varieties flowering throughout the year (but mainly either summer or winter) – in shades of pink, purple, red and white (some have yellow or orange foliage). Trim the plants over after flowering. **Note:** Heathers must be grown in ericaceous compost. *See also Calluna*.
H 25 cm (10 in), S 25 cm (10 in)

Fatsia japonica
An evergreen shrub with large hand-like, glossy leaves. It collapses after a frost but generally recovers. Ideal for a sheltered shady spot.
H 1.5 m (5 ft), S 1 m (3 ft)

Fuchsia
There are hundreds of fuchsia varieties, with flowers – carried from summer to autumn – in shades of pink, red and purple. Trailing forms are ideal for hanging baskets. Most can be stored (leafless) over winter in a frost-free place for use the following year.
H 30 cm (12 in), S 30 cm (12 in)

Hebe pinguifolia
While many hebes are best in borders, several make neat evergreen domes that are ideal for containers. Types with variegated leaves provide year-round interest. Summer flowers (attractive to bees) are white, pink, blue or purple.
H 60 cm (24 in), S 60 cm (24 in), more or less, depending on the variety.

Hedera
Ivy

Evergreen climbers that are invaluable for trailing at the edge of a container or for training upwards on canes. There are many forms with yellow or white patterning on the leaves.
H 30 cm (12 in) or more, S 30 cm (12 in) or more.

Helichrysum
These grey-leaved shrubs are compact and combine well with more flamboyant flowering plants. *Helichrysum petiolare* has trailing stems and is ideal at the edge of a large container or in a hanging basket.
H 30 cm (12 in), S 30 cm (12 in), more or less, depending on the variety.

Hebe pinguifolia

Hydrangea

Hydrangeas make ideal container plants, thriving in partial shade, provided they are kept well watered. Flower colours include white, pink and blue. Blue varieties often have to be watered with a special compound to maintain the colour.
H 60 cm (24 in), S 60 cm (24 in)

Jasminum

Jasmine
The hardy jasmines are mainly deciduous climbers with (sometimes scented) white or yellow flowers. Most need some support, but winter jasmine (*Jasminum nudiflorum*) can be allowed to cascade from a large barrel or similar-sized container. Prune jasmines after flowering.
H 2 m (6 ft), S 1.2 m (4 ft)

Lathyrus odoratus

Sweet pea
Annual climbers with (often) sweetly scented flowers carried in succession throughout summer in shades of white, pink, red, blue and purple. Most should be trained on canes but a few are very compact and need little if any support. Dead-head frequently to maintain flowering.
H 1.2 m (5 ft), S 45 cm (18 in), some forms being much neater growing

Laurus nobilis

Bay
Clipped bays can look very smart in formal designs or to mark a focal point. Small plants can be used in mixed herb plantings. Some protection from severe cold may be necessary. Clip over to shape in spring and summer. H 1.1 m (4 ft), S 60 cm (2 ft), more or less, depending on pruning

Lavandula

Lavender
With their white, lilac or blue summer flowers (very attractive to bees), lavenders are essential cottage-garden plants. The grey foliage can be clipped more formally to shape, but the flowering will not be so good.
H 45 cm (18 in), S 30 cm (12 in)

Lavandula (lavender)

Ligustrum

Privet
Widely used as evergreen hedging, privet is always attractive when clipped to shape for use in large containers, particularly when

grown as a standard. Some forms have golden or variegated leaves.
H 1.1 m (4 ft), S 1 m (3 ft), more or less, depending on pruning

Lonicera nitida
A small-leaved shrub that can be used in place of box. 'Baggesen's Gold' has bright yellow leaves. Clip regularly to keep neat. H 30 cm (12 in), S 30 cm (12 in), more without pruning

Musa basjoo
Banana palm
For a tropical or colonial look, this architectural plant is unrivalled. The large paddle-like leaves, which split at the edges, are almost translucent. Protect in winter in frost-prone areas. H 2 m (6 ft), S 1 m (3 ft)

Opuntia ficus-indica
Prickly pear
A large cactus with spiny pads. In warm climates, it can produce yellow flowers and edible fruits. Mature specimens are tree-like with a striking outline. H 2 m (6 ft), S 1.1 m (4 ft)

Phoenix canariensis
Date palm
Small date palms with short trunks make excellent architectural plants for containers.

They need protection from frost in winter.
H 1.1 m (4 ft), S 1 m (3 ft), though potentially much taller

Phyllostachys nigra
Black bamboo
A dramatic bamboo with slim canes that are green initially but turn black as they mature. Container growing usefully limits its spread. H 2.1 m (7 ft), S 1 m (3 ft)

Rhododendron
This large group of plants – which includes azaleas – comprises both dwarf and larger plants, deciduous and evergreen, with white, pink, yellow, red or purple flowers (which can be scented). Some have silver-grey leaves. Prune carefully after flowering (in late winter to mid spring). **Note:** All rhododendrons must be grown in ericaceous compost.
H 75 cm (30 in), S 75 cm (30 in), but size can vary, depending on the variety.

Azalea

Roses

While some roses (*Rosa*), especially the climbers and ramblers, are very vigorous plants that can be difficult to maintain in containers, there is a whole host of others that have been bred for this very purpose. The following can be recommended:

'Anne Boleyn'
Modern shrub rose with large warm pink flowers, best in a large container (1 m/3 ft x 1 m/3 ft).

'Baby Masquerade'
Miniature with yellow flowers that fade to orange and red (30 cm/12 in x 30 cm/12 in).

'Grace'
Modern shrub rose with large apricot flowers, best in a large container (1.1 m/4 ft x 1.1 m/4 ft).

'Laura Ford'
Miniature climber with sweetly scented yellow flowers (1.2 m/5 ft x 60 cm/2 ft).

'Northamptonshire'
Groundcover rose with dainty pink flowers. (45 cm/18 in x 100 cm/36 in).

'Queen Mother'
Patio rose with pink flowers that open flat. (45 cm/18 in x 45 cm/18 in)

Note: When planting roses, always be sure to bury the graft union, so the bases of the stems are just below compost level.

Rosmarinus officinalis (rosemary)

Rosmarinus officinalis
Rosemary

Shrubby herby plants with spikes of blue, purple or white flowers in spring and summer. Forms with trailing stems are good in hanging baskets or at the edge of a large container. They can be kept neat with regular clipping.
H 45 cm (18 in), S 45 cm (18 in)

Ruta graveolens
Rue
An attractive shrubby plant with blue-grey leaves. The mustard yellow summer flowers are best removed for the best foliage effect. The leaves are highly aromatic but can cause skin rashes on contact.
H 90 cm (36 in), S 75 cm (30 in)

Salvia officinalis
Sage
Sages can have greyish green, purple or variegated leaves (splashed with pink, purple and cream). The small summer flowers are best removed. Trim regularly to keep plants neat.
H 30 cm (12 in), S 45 cm (18 in)

Sarcococca
Christmas box
Neat-growing shrubs with glossy evergreen leaves and sweetly scented winter flowers. They can be pruned for neatness after flowering, if necessary.
H 60 cm (24 in), S 90 cm (36 in)

Skimmia japonica
These evergreen shrubs make neat domes of foliage and produce sweetly scented cones of white flowers in late winter to early spring. The unopened buds of 'Rubella' are bright pink and are a feature throughout winter.
H 90 cm (36 in), S 90 cm (36 in)

Syringa
Lilac
Most lilacs are too large for most containers, but Syringa persica is a dainty deciduous shrub with pyramids of scented purple flowers in late spring. Prune carefully after flowering, if necessary.
H 1.1 m (4 ft), S 1.1 m (4 ft)

Tamarix
Tamarisk
Deciduous shrubs that are grown for their feathery leaves and frothy pink flowers (which appear in late spring or summer, depending on the variety). Prune spring-flowering types just after flowering, late-flowering ones in early spring.
H 2 m (6 ft), S 1.1 m (4 ft)

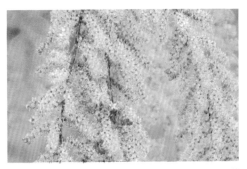

Tamarix (tamarisk)

Taxus
Yew

Often used for hedging, these evergreen conifers can also be grown in containers and kept compact with regular clipping.
H 2 m (6 ft), S 60 cm (2 ft), more or less, depending on severity of pruning.

Trachelospermum
Star jasmine

An evergreen climber with deliciously scented starry white flowers that appear throughout summer and into autumn (when the leaves often turn red). It needs a sheltered sunny position.
H 1.2 m (5 ft), S 60 cm (2 ft)

Trachycarpus fortunei
Chusan palm

The hardiest of the palms and ideal for giving a tropical look to any planting. The fan-like leaves end in sharp points.
H 1.2 m (5 ft), S 1 m (3 ft), but capable of growing taller.

Yucca gloriosa
Spanish dagger

These strongly architectural plants have rosettes of long blade-like leaves (some varieties are variegated) and tall spires of creamy white flowers in late summer. Mature specimens can become tree-like.
H 1.2 m (5 ft), S 1 m (3 ft)

Perennials and Grasses

Aeonium 'Zwartkop'
This succulent plant – also good as a houseplant – is like a mini tree, with rosettes of dark chocolate purple leaves. It needs winter protection in frost-prone areas.
H 45 cm (18 in), S 45 cm (18 in)

Agapanthus
These perennials thrive in containers, flowering best (in shades of blue and occasionally white) when pot bound.
H 60 cm (24 in), S 30 cm (12 in)

Agapanthus

Athyrium nipponicum 'Pictum'
Japanese painted fern

One of the prettiest ferns, with fronds that are delicately marked with purple and silver. It needs ericaceous compost.
H 20 cm (8 in), S 20 cm (8 in)

Aubrieta

Vivid blue or purple flowers cover these compact perennials in spring. Trim them back after flowering to keep neat.
H 5 cm (2 in), S 30 cm (12 in)

Ballota

Shrubby Mediterranean perennials that are grown more for their felted grey leaves – carried on upright stems – than for their tiny purple summer flowers.
H 45 cm (18 in), S 60 cm (24 in)

Brunnera

These perennials are grown less for their blue spring flowers than for their handsome leaves, sometimes dramatically marked with white, cream or silver.
H 45 cm (18 in), S 45 cm (18 in)

Chrysanthemum

Valued for their late flowers, in shades of white, pink, yellow, orange and red. Some are not hardy, so need winter protection.
H 45 cm (18 in), S 45 cm (18 in), more or less, depending on the variety.

Cortaderia selloana

Pampas grass
With its tall plumes of late summer flowers, which last through winter, this is one of the most impressive of the grasses. Needs a large container. Variegated forms are more compact.
H 2 m (6 ft), S 1 m (3 ft)

Crambe maritima

Sea kale
The blue-grey leaves are thick and drought-resistant. White flowers appear in early summer.
H 45 cm (18 in), S 45 cm (18 in)

Eryngium

Sea holly
Architectural plants with spiny edged whitish grey leaves (sometimes on blue stems) and bright blue or purple flowers.
H 45 cm (18 in), S 45 cm (18 in), more or less, depending on the variety.

Chrysanthemums

Helleborus

Hellebore

Hellebores are valued for their late winter flowers and handsome evergreen foliage. Flower colours are white, warm pink, cream, yellow and purple.

H 25 cm (10 in), S 25 cm (10 in)

Heuchera

Excellent shade plants with interesting foliage – sometimes yellow, chocolate purple or intriguingly marbled. Early summer flowers, on tall spires, are a bonus.

H 30 cm (12 in), S 30 cm (12 in)

Hosta

Handsome foliage plants with leaves that can be plain green, bright yellow-green, blue-grey (and usually thick-textured) or generously splashed or margined with white, cream or yellow. The summer flowers (white, lilac or purple) are incidental.

H to 90 cm (36 in), S to 90 cm (36 in), though some forms are more compact.

Miscanthus

Deciduous or evergreen grasses that make a graceful effect in containers, with arching leaves and plumes of flowers from late summer to autumn.

H 1.2 m (5 ft), S 1 m (3 ft), more or less, depending on the type.

Ophiopogon planiscapus 'Nigrescens'

A clump-forming, neat-growing, grassy perennial with dramatic, black-purple leaves. It also has white flowers in summer.

H 20 cm (8 in), S 20 cm (8 in)

Paeonia

Peony

Beautiful perennials grown for their sumptuous early-summer flowers (usually white, pink or red, sometimes yellow or orange) and foliage that turns red in autumn. Most need staking.

H 60 cm (24 in), S 60 cm (24 in)

Phormium

New Zealand flax

Dramatic evergreen with blade-like leaves, sometimes striped or margined with cream, red, pink or purple. Tall flower spikes sometimes appear in summer.

H 2 m (6 ft), when in flower, S 1 m (3 ft)

Primula polyanthus group

Essential plants for winter and spring containers, with clusters of flowers in bright colours – white, cream, pink, yellow, red, blue and orange –

sometimes with contrasting centres.
H 15 cm (6 in), S 20 cm (8 in)

Scabiosa 'Ace of Spades'

Dramatic blackish purple pincushion-like
flowers appear on tall wiry stems in summer.
H 60 cm (24 in), S 60 cm (24 in)

Sedum spectabile

The icy-looking succulent leaves make firm
mounds before heads of white, pink or brick
red flowers (which are attractive to bees)
appear in late summer and autumn.
H 30 cm (12 in), S 30 cm (12 in)

Sempervivum

Houseleeks

Houseleeks have clustering rosettes of thick
fleshy, pointed leaves, usually greyish green
but sometimes tipped with maroon or brown.
Excellent in a shallow container in full sun.
H 10 cm (4 in), S 15 cm (6 in), or more.

Stachys lanata

Bunnies' ears

Softly hairy leaves are silvery grey (some
forms having soft yellow leaves) – an excellent
foil to other plants. Insignificant purple flowers
sometimes appear in hot weather in summer.
H 15 cm (6 in), S 30 cm (12 in), or more.

Stipa gigantea

Golden oats

This evergreen grass makes a bold clump of
arching leaves topped with upright spikes of
silver flowers in summer and autumn.
H 2 m (6 ft) when in flower, S 1 m (3 ft)

Tiarella

Foam flower

Dainty but robust perennials with leaves that
can be splashed or tinged with yellow, orange
or purple. Spikes of white or pink flowers
appear in spring to summer.
H 30 cm (12 in), S 30 cm (12 in)

Sedum spectabile

Bulbs

Canna

Indian shot plant

Dramatic leaves, sometimes boldly striped, offset the spikes of yellow, orange or red flowers that appear in summer to early autumn. In cold areas, store the bulbs dry over winter.

H 1 m (3 ft), S 30 cm (12 in)

Crocosmia 'Lucifer'

The best of the crocosmias, with pleated fan-like leaves and bold spikes of tomato-red flowers in summer.

H 1 m (3 ft), S 60 cm (2 ft)

Crocus

Essential spring bulbs with goblet-like flowers in shades of white, cream, yellow, lilac and purple.

H 10 cm (4 in), S 5 cm (2 in)

Cyclamen

These winter-flowering bulbs have flowers with upswept petals in shades of white, pink and red. Store the bulbs dry over summer.

H 15 cm (6 in), S 15 cm (6 in)

Dahlia

Flowers, which appear from summer to autumn, range in size and shape, varying in colour from white, pink and red to yellow and orange. Dry the bulbs after flowering for storage over winter.

H 1 m (3 ft), S 30 cm (12 in), more or less, depending on the variety.

Hyacinthus

Hyacinth

Hypnotically scented plants for late spring with flowers in white, pink, yellow, orange or blue. Forced bulbs – for indoor use – will flower earlier.

H 20 cm (8 in), S 12.5 cm (5 in)

Iris

Dwarf irises – especially winter-flowering types – are ideal for shallow containers. *Iris danfordiae* has yellow flowers, while those of *I. reticulata* are dark blue splashed with yellow.

H 10 cm (4 in), S 5 cm (2 in)

Cyclamen

Lilium
Lily
Beautiful plants for summer interest. There are many hybrids, with white, pink, yellow, red or orange flowers or stick to reliable *Lilium regale*, with white scented flowers.
H 45 cm (18 in), S 15 cm (6 in), more or less, depending on the variety.

Narcissus
Daffodil
There are hundreds of daffodil varieties, all with white, cream or (most commonly) yellow flowers. Dwarf varieties, usually early spring flowering, are best for containers, though all are suitable.
H 30 cm (12 in), S 10 cm (4 in), more or less, depending on the variety.

Tulipa
Tulip
Tulips produce richly saturated colours – white, pink, yellow, red or orange – in late spring. Some varieties combine more than one colour.
H 30 cm (12 in), S 10 cm (4 in), more or less, depending on the variety.

Tulipa (tulip)

Annuals
Unless otherwise stated, all the following flower in summer to early autumn.

Ageratum
Floss flower
Compact plants that smother themselves with fluffy blue flowers.
H 10 cm (4 in), S 10 cm (4 in)

Angelonia
Tender perennial with snapdragon-like white, blue or violet flowers over a long period.
H 45 cm (18 in), S 30 cm (12 in)

Arctotis
These plants produce daisy flowers in white, pink, yellow, orange or purple, which are often strikingly marked with contrasting colours.
H 30 cm (12 in), S 30 cm (12 in)

Arctotis

Bacopa
White, blue or purple flowers are produced over a long period. It needs frequent watering and feeding with a seaweed extract.
H 10 cm (4 in), S 30 cm (12 in)

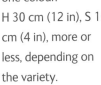

Begonia

Essential flowers for shade, colours
being white, pink, yellow, orange and red.
Some forms are compact. 'Tuberous'
types have trailing stems and are good
in hanging baskets.
H 20 cm (8 in), S 30 cm (12 in), trailing types
having a greater spread.

Calceolaria

Slipper flower
Intriguing pouch-like flowers – yellow, red,
orange or purple, and sometimes marked
with different colours – are produced over
a long period.
H 25 cm (10 in), S 30 cm (12 in)

Cosmos

Easily raised from seed, these plants have
papery poppy-like flowers in shades of white,
pink, crimson or maroon.
H 45 cm (18 in), S 30 cm (12 in)

Cuphea

Tubular bright coral-red flowers stand out
against the foliage.
H 30 cm (12 in), S 30 cm (12 in), or more.

Eschscholzia

California poppy

These easy-to-grow plants have fluted
flowers in shades of mainly orange, but
sometimes white, pink, yellow or red. Some
varieties have double flowers.
H 25 cm (10 in), S 10 cm (4 in)

Felicia

Blue daisy
Tender perennial
with masses of
(usually) blue or
white daisy flowers
over a long period.
H 30 cm (12 in), S
30 cm (12 in), or
more. Variegated
forms are more
compact.

Felicia (blue daisy)

Gazania

Large, bright orange daisy flowers open fully
in sun, closing up in cloudy weather.
H 20 cm (8 in), S 25 cm (10 in)

Glechoma

A perennial with creeping stems, used to trail
and add contrast to flowering plants in large
containers and hanging baskets. Variegated
forms are the most popular.
H 15 cm (6 in), S 90 cm (36 in)

Helianthus
Sunflower
Some sunflower varieties are compact and ideal for containers. Colours are mainly yellow, though sometimes cream, orange or red.
H 40 cm (16 in), S 20 cm (8 in) (dwarf forms.)

Impatiens
Busy Lizzie
Reliable flowerers for a shady area, colours including white, pink, orange and red. New Guinea types have darker exotic-looking leaves.
H 20 cm (8 in), S 20 cm (8 in), more or less.

Lobelia
Compact or trailing plants that produce masses of usually blue, or white or red flowers. They tolerate some shade.
H 10 cm (4 in), S 15 cm (6 in), trailing forms having a greater spread.

Lotus berthelottii
Trailing stems are clothed with silvery needle-like leaves. They sometimes carry claw-like red flowers during hot periods.
H 30 cm (12 in), S 60 cm (24 in) or more.

Matthiola
Stock
Usually sweetly fragrant flowers in white, pink, mauve, purple or violet. Some forms have double flowers. H 30 cm (12 in), S 25 cm (10 in)

Matthiola incana (stock)

Mesembryanthemum
Livingstone daisy
Low-growing plants with daisy flowers in shades of white, pink and orange. The flowers open only in full sun.
H 10 cm (4 in), S 20 cm (8 in)

Myosotis
Forget-me-not
The blue (occasionally white) flowers appear in spring on branching stems. An ideal companion to tulips and other spring bulbs.
H 15 cm (6 in), S 15 cm (6 in), more or less, depending on the variety.

Nicotiana
Tobacco plant
Deliciously fragrant white, pink, red or lime-green flowers open to release their scent at night. During hot weather, they often droop.
H 30 cm (12 in), S 15 cm (6 in)

Osteospermum

This tender perennial produces a succession of daisies (sometimes with spoon-shaped petals) in shades of white, cream and shining purple. H 45 cm (18 in), S 45 cm (18 in)

Pelargonium

These tender perennials, of which there are many varieties, have red, pink or white flowers. Types with trailing stems are ideal for window boxes and hanging baskets. Scented-leaf varieties are grown more for their scent and may have insignificant flowers. H 30 cm (12 in), S 30 cm (12 in), trailing varieties having a greater spread

Petunia

Trumpet-like flowers, sometimes with frilly edges, can be white, cream, pink, red or blue. Some are attractively striped or edged with white. H 30 cm (12 in), S 15 cm (6 in)

Petunia

Tagetes

French and African marigolds Compact plants with single or frilly pompom-like yellow or orange flowers. Some forms are marked with red. H 20 cm (8 in), S 20 cm (8 in), more or less, depending on the variety.

Tropaeolum majus

Nasturtium Compact or trailing plants with usually orange but sometimes red or yellow flowers. Some forms have marbled leaves. H 30 cm (12 in), S 45 cm (18 in), some forms having a greater spread.

Verbena

These tender perennials can be branching or bushy but all have an abundance of posy-like flowers in white, pink, red, blue or purple. H 25 cm (10 in), S 25 cm (10 in)

Viola

Winter pansies Winter pansies are essential for giving colour to winter containers. Flower colours include white, cream, yellow, orange and blue. Flowers can be marked with contrasting colours. H 15 cm (6 in), S 15 cm (6 in)

Zinnia

Dwarf compact forms, mainly with yellow, orange or red flowers, are ideal for containers. 'Envy' has green flowers and tolerates shade. H 20cm (8 in), S 20 cm (8 in)

Zinnia

Checklist

Spring

☑ **Seasonal impact:** For an instant display, buy small plants in flower from a garden centre.

☑ **Bulbs:** Many bulbs flower in spring – choose from crocuses, dwarf daffodils, muscari, tulips, fritillaries and hyacinths.

☑ **Successional planting:** Bulbs planted for flowering in succession will provide interest over many weeks.

☑ **Feed bulbs:** If you want to keep bulbs after flowering, feed them before they die back.

Summer

☑ **Annuals and perennials:** For plenty of colour throughout the summer months, use annuals and tender perennials. Use foliage plants as a foil to the flowers.

☑ **Continuous blooms:** Roses, fuchsias and pelargoniums will also flower throughout summer.

Autumn

☑ **Berries:** Use berrying plants to provide colour, as summer plants will start producing fewer flowers.

☑ **Propagate:** Take cuttings of tender perennials to provide plants for next year. Cuttings can be rooted in water indoors.

☑ **Camellias:** Keep watering camellias in containers.

Winter

☑ **Scent:** Many winter-flowering shrubs have sweetly scented flowers.

☑ **Colour:** For colourful flowers, use heathers, hellebores, cyclamen, winter pansies and polyanthus primroses.

☑ **Evergreens:** Combine flowering plants with dwarf evergreen shrubs and conifers.

Year-round Interest

☑ **Variegated plants:** Use variegated evergreen shrubs and conifers for colour throughout the year. They can be underplanted with other plants for seasonal interest.

Containers For Special Places

shade

Many plants are adapted to shady conditions and some of these also thrive in containers. It's easy to create colourful and stylish plantings for not-so-sunny parts of the garden, or a patio that's often screened by the house.

Benefits of Shade

A shady part of the garden can seem like a cool retreat, especially during hot weather. Foliage plants often do better in shady areas than sunny ones – hot sun can scorch delicate leaves – and so you can create a lush, almost tropical feel. You do not have to do without flowers, however – while most plants flower less freely in shade, the flowers last longer and hold their colour better than they do in hot sun. Slugs thrive in cool, damp, shady sites. Keep an eye out for them and deal with them as soon as you spot any damage (see page 80)

Note: A shady part of the garden offers an ideal spot for resting houseplants during the summer. Not only will these contribute to the scene, but they will benefit from a period outdoors – summer breezes and natural rainfall will firm the growth.

A Taste of the Orient

A shady patio is an ideal site for a Zen or Japanese-style garden. Plant large glazed containers with the shade-loving plants that typify this style – elegant Japanese maples (*Acer japonicum* and *A. palmatum*), dwarf pines (forms of *Pinus mugo*), hostas, grasses and ferns. Bamboos will add height. A few rocks or large pebbles could complete the look.

If you want to add water to enhance the scene, simply place a few shallow bowls around the plants or install a small fountain. Most water plants need full sun, so a water garden as such is not practical.

Top Tip

Paving and decking attracts algae, especially if it does not drain properly. Not only is this unsightly, but it can be slippery underfoot. Wash down with an algicide regularly to keep the area clear.

Acer japnonicum (maple)

Plants for shade

Most evergreen shrubs and conifers that are grown for their overall shape and 'presence' do well in a shady spot. Clip them regularly to keep them neat. Other plants that thrive in shade include:

- *Acer japonicum, A. palmatum* (Japanese maple)
- *Aspidistra elatior* (cast-iron plant)
- *Aucuba japonica* 'Crotonifolia' (Spotted laurel)
- *Buxus* (box)
- *Helleborus* (hellebore)
- *Heuchera*
- *Hosta*
- *Musa basjoo* (banana palm)
- *Tiarella* (foam flower)

Tiarella (foam flower)

Fuchsia

Plants that flower in shade

The following can be relied on to provide colour in a shady spot:

Begonia

Brunnera

Camellia

Fuchsia

Helleborus (hellebore)

Impatiens (busy Lizzie)

Lobelia

Rhododendron

Hostas

Hostas are rightly considered the queen of foliage plants, and there are literally hundreds of varieties to choose from. They all make excellent container plants. For the lushest growth, feed the plants regularly with a seaweed extract. Watch out for slugs, particularly in spring, when the new growth is appearing. For effective methods of control, *see* page 80. Choose from the following:

 Blue leaves: 'Blue Angel', 'Blue Mouse Ears', 'Halcyon' and *H. sieboldiana*

 Yellow leaves: 'Gold Standard', 'Stained Glass' and 'Sum and Substance'

 Variegated leaves: 'Christmas Candy', 'Gypsy Rose', 'Morning Light', 'War Paint' and 'Yellow River'

Ferns

All ferns thrive in shade – most are plants of damp woodland or cool rock faces. Some will even do well in deep shade, sending up elegant fronds each spring. Another plus point is that ferns are virtually slug-proof. When buying ferns, check to see whether they need acid soil – if this is the case, pot them up in ericaceous compost (*see* page 46). Being adapted to growing in damp conditions, ferns will need regular watering, but are easy to feed – a few applications of seaweed extract is usually enough to keep them healthy. For a touch of colour in summer, try combining ferns with red begonias.

Balconies, Roof Gardens and Terraces

Containers come into their own in areas where there is no garden soil. This is one area where you have to give due consideration to the type of container and compost, as these structures will not always carry heavy loads.

Make any balcony or roof terrace – however small – part of your living space. Think of the plants as the soft furnishings that will introduce colour and movement to complement weatherproof outdoor tables and chairs.

Using Containers

If you live in an apartment or studio in a large city – and particularly if you work in an office during the week – you will have limited access to green spaces. Even a shallow balcony can house a multitude of plants, so you can sit out on pleasant evenings and be surrounded by greenery. You can also use plants to screen or distract attention from an unsympathetic view.

A narrow balcony can be home to a surprising number of plants. Make sure that any which sit on the top of a balustrade or railing are firmly fixed in position to avoid nasty accidents.

Roof gardens pose particular – but not insurmountable – problems. These can be relatively large spaces, often with spectacular views over streets and neighbouring buildings. With containers, you can transform a roof space into a real 'garden in the air'.

Balconies

Balconies always have railings or walls that define the space (as well as stopping you from falling off). You can fix window boxes on both sides of these, thus doubling up on the use of available space. This allows you to grow plants on the inside and also plants that will cascade out (to provide interest at street level).

A balcony can house so many plants that you can easily forget the absence of garden soil. Here, the top growth of adjacent plants has knitted together to create almost a hedge – good shelter from prying eyes.

Aspect

Balconies present the gardener with certain specific issues that affect plant growth.

Heat: They are usually very sheltered. If they face the sun all day, they can be veritable sun traps.

Rain shadow: The wall of the building will also shelter the plants from rainfall (especially if there are overhanging balconies on floors above). Regular watering therefore becomes very important.

Light: Since the light is directional (i.e. cut off by the walls), you will have to turn plants regularly to ensure even growth – otherwise the stems will all grow towards the light.

Warmth: Depending on how high above ground level you are, frosts are less likely to cause a problem (as cold air sinks, the air temperature will always be fractionally higher the higher up you are).

Watering

There is unlikely to be a source of water on a balcony, and installing a water butt is impractical. You may need to make several visits to the kitchen or bathroom sink with a watering can to meet the plants' needs. If you can, move plants around when it's raining (to make sure they all benefit) and/or choose plants that tolerate dry conditions.

Roof Gardens

Being on a roof – particularly if the building is a tall one – can sometimes feel like travelling on an open-top bus. It's windy up there. Access can also be problematic, and you may have to restrict your choice to small plants that are easily carried up flights of stairs. However, it may be possible to install a water butt to collect rainwater, so you will always have a source of water for the plants.

Shade and Shelter

A roof garden is generally exposed to all the elements. Plants can bake in hot weather and will easily blow over in strong winds. You may need to erect a windbreak, comprising a green mesh stretched between uprights that are securely attached to the building. Screening fabrics effectively filter wind while allowing some sunlight and rain to pass through – they will also shelter you from prying eyes from neighbouring rooftops. You can, of course, also use wooden trellis panels. For more information on container plants for a windy site, *see* page 181. For plants for full sun, *see* page 184.

Choosing Containers

The important thing to remember is that you need to keep the weight of the containers on balconies and roof gardens as low as possible to limit possible wear on the building. Look for lightweight plastic or fibreglass containers – it will also be easier to move these around the space once planted.

A Nice Set of Wheels

When buying your containers, it's also well worth investing in some wheeled platforms or stands of matching size. With these, you'll be able to move the containers around at will.

Composts

A balcony or roof garden is a situation where multi-purpose and coir-based composts come into their own – as they are much lighter in weight than loam-based composts. To further reduce weight, replace up to one third of the compost with perlite or vermiculite. In place of large stones or crocks at the base of each container, substitute chunks of polystyrene.

Note: Since you'll be using lightweight composts – which are often low in nutrients – out of necessity, it is doubly important to feed the plants well with an appropriate fertilizer applied at regular intervals while they are growing strongly.

Vertical Gardening

Vertical gardening offers the ideal solution for plant lovers who have very limited space. In a sense, it is an extension of the principle behind hanging baskets – plants are suspended on walls.

Systems

Etagères and plant stands offer a form of vertical gardening (see page 60), but it's possible to take this idea even further. You can use every available wall – not only garden and house walls, but also garage walls, balcony walls, shed walls and fence panels.

Dedicated frames are designed to accommodate growbags (the type that are often used for growing tomatoes and other fruiting vegetables). The bags are inserted in the frame edge and the plants grow through holes in the frames.

Other models are more sophisticated. The plants are supported on a grid incorporating a watering system that takes moisture directly to the roots of each plant. Conventional compost – which is heavy and can put a strain on the support – is replaced by a lightweight felt, and nutrients essential for plant growth are delivered in the water supply. (This system of growing plants is a form of hyrdoponics – in which compost is replaced by an inert system and plants are kept growing with a liquid feed.)

Plants for Vertical Gardens

Bearing in mind that conditions for growth are not ideal, permanent plants should be chosen with care – they may need to withstand drought, extreme temperatures, high light intensity and strong wind. Look for plants adapted to cope with these harsh conditions. Perennial plants suitable for vertical gardening include:

Sedum acre (stonecrop)

- *Anthyllis vulneraria* (kidney vetch)
- *Centaurea scabiosa* (greater knapweed)
- *Echium vulgare* (viper's bugloss)
- *Hieracium lanatum* (leafy hawkweed)
- *Knautia macedonica* (field scabious)
- *Linaria vulgaris* (toadflax)
- *Lotus corniculatus* (bird's foot trefoil)
- *Origanum vulgare* (wild marjoram)
- *Primula veris* (cowslip)
- *Sedum acre* (stonecrop)
- *Trifolium pratense* (clover)

Echium vulgare (viper's bugloss)

Fruit and Vegetables

A vertical allotment can be surprisingly productive. Varieties that are described as 'dwarf', 'trailing' or 'compact' or 'suitable for hanging baskets' can all be grown in this way. Besides many varieties of strawberry and tomato, 'Baby Doll' aubergines, 'Slenderette' dwarf beans and petits pois can be successful. Herbs and leafy vegetables are also worth trying. Plant lettuces, rocket and sorrel for leaves. Among herbs, creeping and mat-forming thymes are particularly recommended, alongside annuals such as basil and parsley.

Summer Flowers

Many traditional hanging basket plants can provide colour in summer if grown in this way – especially petunias (look out for mini varieties), trailing pelargoniums, nemesias and verbenas, lobelia and alyssum. Trim over with scissors periodically to dead-head and keep up the flowering display.

Windy Spots

Wind is the enemy of nearly all garden plants – much more so than cold or heat. Strong winds scorch leaves, especially delicate ones, and inhibit strong upright growth. Fortunately, there are plants that tolerate windy situations, and several thrive in containers.

Choosing Plants

Plants that grow on the sides of mountains or in open moorland in the wild are well adapted to having the air blowing through their stems. These harsh conditions have a dwarfing effect, and they generally hug the ground. This actually makes them ideal for container gardening, as they are seldom over-vigorous and can stay in their containers for several years.

Choosing Containers

This is where terracotta and stone containers are the obvious choice, as, being heavy for their size even before they are planted, they are much less likely to blow over. You can increase their solidity by lining the base with heavy bricks or stones, especially if you are choosing a large plant that may be top heavy.

Note: Heavy containers are not recommended for use on a windy balcony or roof garden, as it's advisable to limit the load on the structure. Lightweight containers may have insufficient ballast, however. Make sure they do not blow over and secure them firmly to an available support – the ground, a wall or railings – so they won't go crashing to the ground in a gale.

Countering Wind

You can lessen the effect of wind by creating a suitable windbreak that will shelter less tolerant plants. If necessary, use windbreak fabric as recommended for roof gardens (*see* page 175) – these are seldom obtrusive once there are plants in front of them. Some plants themselves will effectively filter the wind. Bamboos and tall grasses in containers will do the job perfectly, and contribute to the scene positively as the wind rustles through their stems.

Plants that Tolerate Wind

Aubrieta

Berberis

Buxus (box)

Calluna and Erica (heathers)

Hebe pinguifolia

Lonicera nitida

Pinus mugo

Rosmarinus (rosemary)

Tamarix (tamarisk)

Taxus (yew)

Aubrieta

Calluna (heather)

Grasses and Bamboos for a Windy Site

Arundo donax

Cortaderia selloana (pampas grass)

Miscanthus

Phyllostachys

Stipa gigantea (golden oats)

Suntraps

The suntrap garden – bathed for hours in sunlight – sounds idyllic, but while it's a dream for sun-worshippers, it does create certain issues for the plants. Fortunately, there are some that will thrive and positively relish a good roasting.

Containers

This is one situation where your choice of container can have a marked effect on plant growth. Plastic and metal both tend to heat up alarmingly in full sun, and plant roots can bake. Thick terracotta or stone will help keep plant roots cool. If you must use lightweight containers – on a balcony or roof terrace, for instance – look for synthetics with a shiny white or cream finish. These will reflect light back, absorbing less than matt black or dark-coloured ones, with a lower risk of overheating.

If you can devise a method of shading the containers, so much the better. Positioning them near low walls or hedges, or simply grouping them together, will help lower the temperature around the roots.

Top Tip

Use stems of rosemary and lavender to scent a bed linen drawer – or fling them into an evening bath to reduce stress.

Compost

Plants adapted to drought seldom like to be kept wet at the roots. Well-drained potting compost is essential. Add grit or sand to the compost (or perlite or vermiculite, if you need to keep the weight down), replacing up to around a third. Top-dress the compost surface with grit or marble chippings – this will not only keep the roots cool but also reflect light back on to the leaves.

Watering and Feeding

Most drought-loving plants have low nutrient requirements, and feeding should not be necessary as they can produce their own food from sunlight. Water the plants in the evening during hot spells, so that the compost does not dry out excessively.

Did You Know?

Many plants that have been bred for their flowering potential can be disappointing in very hot conditions – the flowers fade too quickly and run to seed.

Mediterranean Style

Many Mediterranean plants thrive in full sun, particularly woody herbs such as lavender (*Lavandula*), rosemary (*Rosmarinus*), sage (*Salvia*) and artemisias. The stems and leaves contain aromatic oils that are released in hot weather. All thrive in containers. Use terracotta or stone and top the compost with grit or stone chippings. The flowers of all these plants are very attractive to bees. On a still afternoon in summer, a suntrap garden will be alive with these valuable pollinators.

Plants for suntrap gardens

Plants with swollen, fleshy and/or hairy leaves are adapted to survive drought, as these act as a water store or have a coating that prevents moisture from evaporating from the leaves. Needing little water, many can be grown in shallow pans, using gritty compost.

Suntrap Plants

Plants adapted to drought

Aeonium

Agave

Ballota

Crambe maritima (sea kale)

Echeveria

Eryngium (sea holly)

Opuntia (prickly pear)

Sedum spectabile

Sempervivum (houseleek)

Stachys lanata (bunnies' ears)

Crambe maritima (sea kale)

Flowering plants for hot conditions

The following will flower reliably in full sun:

Cosmos

Agapanthus (African lily)

Cosmos

Dahlia

Felicia (blue daisy)

Gazania

Helianthus (sunflower)

Mesembryanthemum (Livingstone daisy)

Osteospermum

Pelargonium

Petunia

Verbena

Zinnia

Checklist

Shade: In a shady spot, major on luscious foliage plants to create a tropical feel. Add colour with shade-tolerant flowering plants such as begonias, impatiens and fuchsias.

Damp: Watch out for algae and mosses that proliferate in shady areas, especially if they are prone to damp.

Slugs: Control slugs, which thrive in cool shady situations.

Weight: On balconies and roof gardens, choose lightweight containers and use a lightweight soil-less compost, further lightened through the addition of perlite or vermiculite. Chunks of polystyrene make better drainage material than crocks or stones.

Screening: On exposed roof gardens, use screening fabrics to filter wind.

Moving pots: Invest in a wheeled platform that will make it easy to move plants around at will.

Vertical planting: If space is limited, consider making use of the walls for vertical planting solutions.

Wind: In windy areas, choose from heavy stone or terracotta containers planted with wind-tolerant plants.

Sun: In a hot suntrap garden, use drought-tolerant plants. Feed them only when necessary, as these plants often have a low nutrient requirement.

Productive Containers

Growing Your Own Food

Many gardeners are interested in growing at least some of their own food, whether it's only a few leafy vegetables or a handful of berries or herbs to add flavour to cooking and salads. Even without a vegetable garden, it is possible to grow edible crops – in containers. With a bit of planning, you can enjoy produce from containers over a long period, from early spring to the first frosts.

Benefits of Home-grown Crops

Growing your own crops has many advantages. Fruit, vegetables and herbs grown at home will all have a much better flavour than anything you can buy in a supermarket, partly because you can always be sure it has been freshly harvested.

Commercial growers look for varieties that produce uniform crops that store well, tolerate transportation and have a long shelf life. Flavour is a secondary concern. Amateur growers have a much wider choice.

You also need no longer worry about your carbon footprint. Supermarket produce has often travelled vast distances. Yours can be – almost literally – on your doorstep.

Crops Without a Garden

Even with the minimum space, you can still enjoy food you've grown yourself. Window boxes can accommodate leafy vegetables and herbs. Even in shade, you can grow lettuces and rocket. There are also varieties of tomato and some strawberries – miniature, but with trailing stems – that have been developed for growing in hanging baskets. Either grow them on their own, or combine them with more traditional hanging-basket plants.

Crops Indoors

A sunny windowsill indoors is the ideal place for growing annual herbs such as basil, parsley and coriander. Grow them from seed or pot up small growing plants from the supermarket.

You can even grow tomatoes, treating the windowsill as a mini greenhouse. Look for dwarf bush varieties that will not grow too tall. Chilli peppers also make an ideal indoor crop, as they are tolerant of high temperatures.

Growing Vegetables

Most vegetables are annual plants that are grown from seed sown each year. If you don't have time to raise your own plants, buy small ones from garden centres in early spring.

Choosing Varieties

Quick-maturing crops are the easiest to grow in pots. Look out especially for compact or dwarf varieties – which have often been developed with container gardening in mind. Look through seed packets in a garden centre or go online – a wider range is available via the internet.

F1 Hybrids

Two seed strains are developed, each with a desirable characteristic, such as disease resistance or size of plant. These are then crossed with each other to produce seeds that will inherit both characteristics alongside 'hybrid vigour'. This is the 'first generation' – hence F_1 hybrids. F_1 hybrids always germinate readily and produce reliable crops. Although more expensive than ordinary seeds, they are worth the extra outlay.

Growing Vegetables from Seed

Seeds are normally packaged in small foil packets inside a larger paper packet (which generally has sowing instructions on the back). To prevent having a glut of a particular crop, make successive sowings over a period of weeks. After cutting open the foil packet, sow only the amount needed for the first crop. Fold over the cut end, then store this (in the outer packet, for identification) in the salad compartment of the refrigerator.

Note: Most seed should be sown as soon as possible, however. If stored for a long period (more than six months), germination will not be so good.

Sowing Seed

Always sow seed as thinly as you can. Crowded seedlings will not be so vigorous and may not grow evenly.

 Compost: Fill pots, trays or modules with seed or multi-purpose compost.

 Water: Lightly firm the compost surface down to level, water (from a watering can fitted with a fine rose, so as not to compact the compost surface) and then allow to drain.

 Seed: Sow the seed thinly and evenly across the compost surface. Cover with the appropriate depth of compost (or sharp sand).

Aftercare

Put the seeds in a light position, but out of direct sunlight. The correct temperature – as indicated on the seed packet – is important. An even temperature, without steep fluctuations, is usually preferred. Spray the compost surface with water every few days so it does not dry out. After germination, turn the container daily, as the seedlings tend to stretch towards the light.

Vegetable seedlings

Pricking Out

When the seedlings produce their second set of leaves, remove them carefully from the compost. Hold them by the leaves, and use a dibber, pencil or the handle of a teaspoon to lift the roots. Pot them up into trays or pots filled with soil-based or multi-purpose compost, allowing more space between them. Water them frequently from now on and feed with a seaweed extract. Pot them on again when they are sturdy and well developed.

Note: If you sowed seed individually in modules, seedlings can stay in the modules until the roots fill them. The seedlings should then be large enough to go outdoors.

Hardening Off

If you raised the seedlings indoors, you will have to acclimatize them to life outside gradually. Stand them outside for increasingly longer periods each day. Be sure to bring them indoors overnight, when it will be colder, particularly if frost is forecast. Hardening off should take about two to three weeks.

Covering Seed

Seed is always sown to its own depth. In other words, if a seed is 20 mm (1 in) in diameter, cover it with 20 mm (1 in) of compost. Very fine seed should just be pressed into the compost surface and then topped with a light sprinkling of compost (it can be easier to use fine sand). Flat seed should be laid flat or, if large enough to handle, pressed into the compost on its edge.

Caring for Your Crops

Most vegetables need a sunny, open site. Leafy vegetables need shade from hot sun to avoid scorching the leaves. In sun, salad crops also tend to produce flowers and seed ('bolting'), which impairs the quality and taste of the leaves. Please bear the following requirements in mind when growing vegetables:

- **Containers:** Choose large containers, ideally at least 25 cm (10 in) deep. The compost is less likely to dry out in these.

- **Compost:** Good-quality compost gives the best results. For preference, use a soil-based compost (John Innes No.2 or No.3). If you use a multi-purpose type, add grit or sharp sand or perlite or vermiculite to improve drainage. Vegetables in multi-purpose compost will need more frequent feeding.

- **Watering and feeding:** Vegetables in pots should be kept well watered at all times. Uneven watering will lead to poor development (and a loss of flavour and texture). Feed vegetables regularly with an organic seaweed extract (or similar product).

Using Growing Bags

These are narrow plastic bags of compost that are intended to be used as they are for growing particular vegetables – usually tomatoes and other salad crops. They are laid flat on the ground and holes are cut in them for the plants. Though convenient to use, they are not things of beauty. They can be concealed with wicker or wooden boxes to improve their appearance – or laid behind small pots of herbs.

Root Vegetables

Most root vegetables are slow-growing, so are unsuitable for containers. However, you will get excellent results from radishes and beetroot. You can make successive sowings to be sure of crops over a long period. Alternatively, beetroot can be harvested when they are the size of golf balls (replace them with a fresh sowing) or you can allow them to grow on to the size of tennis balls. Both are fast-maturing crops, and can be grown in the spaces between other crops (such as lettuces) before these grow too big and crowd them out.

Top Tip

If you need to thin seedlings, rather than discarding them, add them raw to salads.

Leafy Vegetables

Leafy salad crops include all types of lettuce, chard, spinach and rocket. Some of these are very decorative (especially types with red and/or frilly leaves) and can even be used in window boxes and other large containers that are used mainly for flowering plants, especially if you choose cut-and-come-again varieties.

Cut-and-come-again Crops

These are leafy vegetables – including spinach, rocket and some lettuces – that will produce fresh leaves over a long period. Rather than harvesting the whole plant (as is usual), simply remove the leaves you need for immediate use (cutting near the base). Plants will resprout to produce further leaves for cutting.

Potatoes

Perhaps surprisingly, new potatoes are easy to grow in containers, reliably yielding excellent crops. The manner of growing them is quite unique, however. Unlike most other vegetable crops, potatoes are not grown from seed but from special tubers, known (confusingly) as seed potatoes.

Note: Potatoes are not hardy. In cold areas, the stems and leaves should be sheltered from hard frosts. To prevent them from collapsing, lay a length of horticultural fleece over the container on nights when frost is forecast.

Containers

Potatoes need a large deep container. This should preferably be black, as the maximum of light should be excluded, or the tubers may turn green. A black dustbin or compost bin is ideal. Drill holes in the base before use. You can buy special tall containers, specifically for growing potatoes. Some are made of polyethylene or other similar durable fabric and can be folded away after the crop has been harvested for further use next year. They sometimes have a door or flap low down on one side, which you can open in order to harvest the potatoes.

Note: The principle behind container growing for potatoes is to keep raising the level of the compost as the potato plants grow.

Planting and Growing Potatoes

To grow potatoes in a container, follow these simple guidelines:

 Drainage: Fill the base of the container with a layer of crocks, up to 10 cm (4 in) deep, to cover (but not block) the drainage holes.

 Compost: Add a 15 cm (6 in) layer of compost.

 Tubers: Lay five (or more, depending on the size of the container) seed potatoes on the compost surface. Any shoots on the tubers should point upwards. Cover the potatoes with a layer of compost so that they are just covered.

Water in: Water the compost well.

Leaves: When the leaves have grown above the compost surface, add more compost to cover them.

Cover: Keep covering the stems with compost as they grow, until they reach the top of the container.

Harvesting Potatoes

Harvest the potatoes just before the plants come into flower. If there is no door or flap in the side, empty out the container and excavate the potatoes from the compost.

Tomatoes

Because they are so susceptible to disease, tomatoes are nearly always grown in containers, even by gardeners who have dedicated vegetable gardens or allotments. Use individual pots about 25 cm (10 in) in diameter or grow the plants in growing bags (see page 194).

Did You Know?

Technically, tomatoes are fruits, as are aubergines, sweet peppers and chilli peppers. But as they are almost invariably used in savoury dishes, they are often treated as vegetables.

Grafted Tomatoes

Grafting has only recently been applied to tomatoes. Grafted plants are more vigorous than seed-raised ones and produce earlier and bigger crops, with fruiting beginning lower down the stems. They also show greater disease resistance than seed-raised plants. Order plants from a seed merchant or buy them from a garden centre in spring.

Indoors or Outdoors?

Tomatoes are tender plants that do not tolerate frosts. In cold climates, some varieties are suitable for growing outdoors – once all danger of frost has passed – while others should only be grown in a conservatory or greenhouse. Indoor types can be sown in late winter to early spring for early crops. Delay sowing outdoor types till mid spring. By the time the seedlings are well developed, all danger of frost should have passed, and they can be safely placed outside.

Types of Tomato

There is a wide range of fruit size, as detailed below. While most plants produce red fruits, there are also white, orange, yellow and striped varieties.

Four Types of Tomato

Cherry

Slicing

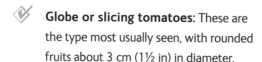

Beefsteak

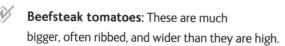

Plum

 Globe or slicing tomatoes: These are the type most usually seen, with rounded fruits about 3 cm (1½ in) in diameter.

Beefsteak tomatoes: These are much bigger, often ribbed, and wider than they are high.

Plum tomatoes: These tomatoes are elongated and often pointed at the tip.

Cherry tomatoes: These are small and round, like marbles.

 Grape tomatoes: Similar to plum tomatoes, but much smaller.

Sowing Tomato Seed

Tomatoes need a temperature of around 20°C (68°F) to germinate. Sow them in trays or small pots. When the seedlings are large enough to handle, pot them up individually into 7.5 cm (3 in) pots and into 12.5 cm (5 in) pots a few weeks later. When they produce their first flowers, they can go into large pots or growing bags. Insert a thin cane or bamboo next to each plant for support.

Training Tomatoes

Tomatoes are usually grown with a single main stem. Pinch out side shoots that appear in leaf joints on the main stem to encourage this to extend upwards. Tie the main stems to the canes as they grow. After the plant has produced four clusters of flowers, pinch out the tip of the main shoot.

Note: Bush varieties do not need to be trained.

Watering and Feeding Tomatoes

Keep tomato plants well watered at all times. Feed the plants regularly with a tomato fertilizer to ensure good fruiting.

Large staked
tomato plant

Top Tip

When in flower, water the plants by spraying over them. This distributes the pollen, ensuring good fruiting.

Growing Fruit

Several fruiting plants thrive in containers, even if you can't create an orchard. But even a few plants can provide a surprisingly large crop.

Site

Most fruit needs sunshine to ripen properly, but the position you choose should be sheltered from strong winds. If you are growing a number of fruiting plants, make sure you stand them with adequate space between them. Too close together and the fruit may not form evenly.

Note: If you can do so, turn the containers during summer, so that the fruits ripen evenly.

Containers

Apart from strawberries, most fruits are produced on bushes and trees, which will be heavy plants when they are laden with fruit. Ideally, choose heavy containers (such as terracotta or wood) that will not blow over in strong winds.

Pollination

Many fruiting plants will only crop reliably if there is another similar plant nearby. When shopping for plants, either buy two or more that are compatible (and will pollinate each other) or look for varieties that are known to be self-fertile and can produce fruit on their own.

Peaches and apricots flower early in the year, before many pollinating insects are active. If you grow one of these, you need to pollinate the plant yourself. On a dry day, collect pollen from an open flower using the tip of a small paintbrush. Dab this over the stamens of a second flower. This mimics the actions of bees and other pollinators.

Compost

Since the plants will be in the containers for several years, choose a good-quality, soil-based compost (John Innes No.3; see page 45). Add grit or sand to improve the drainage. If you opt for multi-purpose compost, you will have to feed more regularly.

Watering and Feeding

Fruiting plants in containers must be kept well watered. Fruit will be shed or may fail to ripen properly if the compost is allowed to dry out. Supplementary feeding, with a potassium-high fertilizer, is also essential. Fork a rose fertilizer (or similar product) into the compost surface in early spring. Water in a tomato fertilizer when the plants are growing strongly.

Note: Most fruiting plants crop between mid summer and autumn. It is important to keep up the watering during this period – so if you're planning a vacation, make sure a friend or neighbour is willing to take on the job in your absence.

A Strawberry Tower

Special containers – usually made of terracotta, which is easily moulded – can be used for growing strawberries in a limited space. Strawberry towers are taller than they are wide, and have special pockets in tiers around the sides. Each pocket will hold one strawberry plant. The fruiting stems trail downwards. For even ripening of the fruit, turn the tower regularly so that all the plants receive equal exposure to the sun.

Top Tip

In a shady spot, try growing alpine strawberries – varieties with tiny but delicious fruits. These are woodland plants that need shelter from full sun.

Apples

Apples can be successfully grown in containers, provided you choose a non-vigorous variety that is recommended for growing in this way. Look for plants that have been trained as dwarf bushes, dwarf pyramids or minarettes (vertical plants with short side shoots). Plants grafted on rootstock M26 usually give good results.

Rootstocks

Many fruit trees are not growing on their own roots but have been grafted on to those of a different plant (the 'rootstock'). Rootstocks influence the way a plant grows and often have a dwarfing effect. They can also promote disease resistance.

Figs

Almost uniquely among fruit trees, figs actually do better in containers than in the open ground. This is because of their extensive root system that enables them to put out quantities of leafy growth – at the expense of fruits. Containers restrict the roots and this greatly benefits fruit production. Choose a large container such as a wooden half-barrel or terracotta pot of similar size.

Although the plants are fully hardy, the fruits need a long hot period to ripen fully. In a cool climate, place the pots against a sunny wall, so the reflected heat will help swell the figs.

Note: While figs can produce two or three crops a year, in frost-prone climates only one per year can ripen fully. Small fruits appear on the stems in late summer. In cold areas, these should be left on the plant to overwinter. They will develop as the following year's crop.

Top Tip

When pruning figs in summer, start at the base of the plant and work your way upwards. The cut stems 'bleed' a white sap. If you start at the top, this will run down on to the stems below.

Pruning Figs

Figs will fruit best if pruned to keep them in bounds. Major pruning is best done in winter. Shorten older stems and any crossing or congested branches (making sure you retain fruit-bearing stems). In summer, remove any newly formed figs (which divert energy from the main crop) and shorten new growth, which is shading the fruits that are now swelling nicely.

Blueberries

Blueberries make ideal container plants. For many gardeners, this is the only way of growing them, as they must have acid soil. The plant itself is highly ornamental, with clusters of bell-like white flowers in spring and excellent leaf colour in autumn – give it a prominent place near the house to appreciate it to the full. For growing in a container, use an ericaceous compost (see page 46), ideally mixed with sharp sand or grit.

Top Tip

The dregs from the teapot and coffee grounds can be tipped over the compost, as they will help keep it acid. Just make sure they are cold first.

Citrus and Olives

In frost-prone areas, these plants are commonly grown for their ornamental value. They are normally pruned regularly to keep them neat and attractive – a practice which actually removes much of the (potentially) fruiting stems. They will usually only fruit successfully (and then not abundantly) if they can be kept in a heated conservatory or greenhouse over winter.

Growing Herbs

Herbs lend themselves to container growing. Compact and neat-growing, a few herbs will not take up much space. They can even be grown in small pots on a kitchen windowsill or in a window box.

Salvia (sage)

Shrubby Herbs

A number of herbs are shrubby evergreens that should be viewed as long-term plants. Rosemary (*Rosmarinus*), lavender (*Lavandula*), sage (*Salvia*), bay (*Laurus*) and thyme (*Thymus*) will all persist from year to year. As they are evergreen, it means that there will always be leaves for picking even in winter.

Perennial Herbs

Perennial herbs are soft-stemmed plants, most of which die back in winter. This group includes mint (*Mentha*), lemon balm (*Melissa*) and chives (*Allium schoenoprasum*).

Did You Know?

Chives grow from bulbs and are related to onions and garlic.

Annual Herbs

Several herbs are annuals that need to be raised from seed each year. Popular annual herbs include parsley (*Petroselinum*), basil (*Ocimum*) and coriander. For sowing seed an dtransplanting seedlings, *see* page 191.

For sowing seed an dtransplanting seedlings, *see* page 191.

Top Tip

If you grow your herbs in their own pots, bring in basil and parsley plants before the first frost. If you keep them on a sunny windowsill and water them regularly, they will carry on producing fresh leaves for a few more weeks.

Growing Basil

Basil seed can be difficult to germinate. It can be easier to buy growing plants from the supermarket. Instead of keeping these on a windowsill indoors (as is intended), pot them up and grow them on outdoors with your other herbs.

Mixing Herbs

Herbs can be grown together in a large single container. A successful combination might include a small bay tree – a standard on a short stem will give you more room for plants underneath – a prostrate rosemary, a sage, some thymes and a few annuals such as basil and parsley.

Note: Mint (*Mentha*) is best grown in a container on its own. It is a spreading, invasive plant that, unlike nearly all the other commonly grown herbs, has a high water requirement and is really best grown in shade.

Site

Most herbs – apart from mint – need a sunny, sheltered position. Hot sun will actually help release the aromatic oils of Mediterranean shrubby herbs such as rosemary and sage.

Mint

Compost

Many herbs do not need a nutrient-high growing medium, but appreciate one that is open and well drained. Always add grit or sharp sand (or perlite or vermiculite) to the compost – whether this is a soil-based John Innes No.2 or multi-purpose compost (*see* page 45).

Watering and Feeding

Water herbs frequently during the growing season (spring to summer) to ensure that the compost does not dry out. In winter, herbs that die back (such as mint) should be watered only to prevent the compost from drying out completely. Most do not need much supplementary feeding, but seaweed extract will help keep them producing plenty of leaves.

Harvesting Herbs

Keep picking leaves from the plants on a regular basis. Not only does this keep the plants neat and compact, but it prevents flower formation. Annual herbs (such as parsley and basil) and chives should not be allowed to flower, as this coarsens the flavour of the leaves.

Parsley

What's the Thyme?

There are many varieties of thyme (*Thymus*), all neat-growing, and many with attractively variegated leaves. Since they are low-growing, with a tendency to spread, they can get swamped by other plants. You can grow several different types together in a shallow pan. Top the compost with grit or stone chippings, as the stems can die back in contact with damp compost. The flowers are very attractive to bees and other pollinating insects.

Note: If you are interested in attracting wildlife, allow a few chives to develop flowers rather than cutting them off. The bright mauve pompoms will bring bees into the garden.

Top Tip

When using bay leaves, to flavour a pâté, casserole or milk pudding, break each leaf in half to release the oils. Rosemary and sage leaves can be lightly crushed using a pestle and mortar.

Drying Herbs

To dry herbs for winter use – or to pass on to friends – cut short stems from the plant. Tie them loosely in bundles with string and then hang them upside down in a warm airy place. Once the stems have dried out, strip the leaves off on to a sheet of paper, then store them in airtight screwtop jars. Rosemary, lavender, sage and bay leaves all dry very successfully. Dry stems of rosemary and lavender can also be used to add fragrance to a linen cupboard.

Note: The flavour of dried herbs is never as strong as that of fresh leaves.

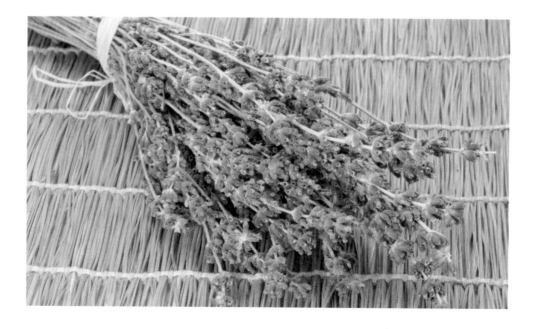

checklist

Seeds: Choose and order suitable vegetable crops from a seed catalogue. Look for dwarf compact varieties. Alternatively, buy small plants from a garden centre.

Container size: Make sure you have suitably sized containers for the plants you are intending to grow.

Save seed: Sow only as much seed as will produce plants for your immediate needs. Save the rest for later sowings so as to have crops over a longer period.

Harvest: Begin harvesting crops such as beetroot while they are young, allowing some to carry on growing.

Care: Feed and water vegetables regularly.Grow leafy crops, such as lettuces, chard and rocket, in a shady site.

Potatoes: Plant seed potatoes in late winter to early spring, in deep containers that you can keep topping up with compost as the potato stems grow.

Tomatoes: Grow tomatoes in individual 25 cm (10 in) pots or growing bags. Train the plants as they grow and keep them well watered and fed.

Fruit: Fruiting plants are usually large, permanent plants, so need a large container and good-quality compost. Prune fig trees for optimum fruiting.

Berries: If space is limited, grow strawberries in a special strawberry tower. Use an ericaceous compost (for lime-hating plants) for blueberries.

Herbs: Keep harvesting leaves from herbs to keep them neat and productive.

Containers Indoors

Indoor Gardening

Houseplants bring life to any interior, even in the depths of winter when plants outdoors are mostly leafless and lifeless – in fact, this is when you will appreciate them most. Most houseplants are very tolerant and easy to care for, and many can be very long-lived. It's easy to get hooked on these plants.

What are Houseplants?

Houseplants are mainly plants from tropical and subtropical regions of the globe. Normally, they cannot be grown outdoors in more temperate regions (where freezing temperatures are common in winter). In their countries of origin – often at or near the equator – day length stays fairly constant through the year and, with no prolonged winter period, plants are more or less permanently in growth. Hence they keep their leaves throughout the year.

A good Rest

While it's theoretically possible to keep houseplants growing year-round, in temperate areas, with long dark winter nights, it's best to allow them to become dormant for around eight to ten weeks during the coldest months.

A Wealth of Choice

Plants can make a significant contribution to your interior design. Whatever the space you have, there are houseplants for you. If you have only a windowsill, there is still plenty of choice, as many are of modest dimensions – such as cacti or African violets (*Saintpaulia*). Trailing plants such as *Tradescantia* or the spider plant (*Chlorophytum*) can find a home on high shelves, from which they will cascade downwards.

Saintpaulia (African violets)

With a conservatory, the sky is – literally – the limit, as there are several taller plants that will reach to the roof. If you have space for larger plants, consider growing trees such as the rubber plant (*Ficus elastica*) or weeping fig (*Ficus benjamina*). The Swiss cheese plant (*Monstera deliciosa*) is a tropical climber that can assume majestic proportions. You could even hang a few baskets among the branches to house yet more plants.

Did You Know?

The Swiss cheese plant gets its name because of the holes in the leaves – like a chunk of Emmental.

Luscious Leaves

Houseplants are predominantly grown for their foliage. While many have simple green leaves – often glossy – others are strikingly variegated. The leaves of many begonias (often sold as *Begonia rex*) are richly patterned with silver, chocolate purple, pink and maroon, often in bold

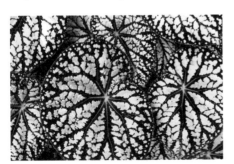

Begonia rex

blotches – the puckered texture is also intriguing. The prayer plant (*Maranta leuconeura*) – so called because it holds its leaves upright, as if in supplication – has foliage that is marked in a herringbone pattern. Mother-in-law's tongue (*Sansevieriea*) has blade-like leaves with pointed tips that are marked with yellow along the edges and have bold silver horizontal bands.

Flowering Houseplants

Some houseplants are grown as much for their attractive flowers as their leaves.

- *Cyclamen persicum*
- *Gardenia*
- *Hoya carnosa* **(wax plant)**
- *Jasminum polyanthum* **(jasmine)**
- **Orchids**
- *Plumbago*
- *Saintpaulia* **(African violet)**
- *Sinningia* **(gloxinia)**
- *Stephanotis*
- *Streptocarpus* **(Cape primrose)**

Cyclamen persicum

Scent Indoors

A few indoor plants have deliciously scented flowers, the most widely grown being jasmine (*Jasminum polyanthum*), gardenias and indoor bulbs such as *Narcissus* 'Paperwhite' and 'Soleil d'Or' and hyacinths (*Hyacinthus*). Be careful where you place these, however. The scent is very strong and can be overpowering, especially in a confined space.

Houseplants with Scented Flowers

Gardenia

Hoya carnosa

Hyacinthus (hyacinth)

Jasminum polyanthum
(jasmine)

Narcissus 'Paperwhite'

Narcissus 'Soleil d'Or'

Stephanotis floribunda

Grouping Plants

While a single large plant can make a striking impression in any interior, you can also devise bold displays by grouping plants together – accentuating contrasts in leaf shapes and habits. This is actually good for the plants. Plants lose water through their leaves, and this transpiration creates a slightly humid microclimate around them, from which they all benefit. It is best to group them together in individual pots rather than growing them all in a single container. Move them around within the group periodically, so that they all have equal access to the light. Plants with large leaves, such as begonias, may start to shade out smaller ones.

Supporting Plants

Since they are not subjected to the buffeting from the elements that plants outdoors put up with, houseplants can be supported with much more delicate frames and canes.

 Hoops: A simple wire hoop – a wire coat hanger bent to shape is the ideal gauge – can be used to support small ivies and other climbers.

 Poles: Some plants produce aerial roots (small roots on the stems, between leaves), and these do well when supported on a moss pole. Twine the stems around the pole as they grow, and the roots will find their own way into the moss. Mist the pole whenever you water.

 Wigwams: Cane or bamboo wigwams can be used as frames for climbers. Use a single central cane to support twiggy plants such as *Ficus benjamina*.

Forced hyacinths

Forced Bulbs

Specially prepared hyacinth bulbs are sold in autumn specifically for growing indoors. They have been treated ('forced') to flower in the middle of winter – eight to twelve weeks before untreated bulbs will flower in the garden. Forced bulbs are often grown in bulb fibre. This is a special low-nutrient mix that also contains charcoal. It can be used in containers without drainage holes – the charcoal prevents the water in the compost from stagnating – hence you can plant up any decorative bowl you happen to own.

 Compost: Partly fill a container with bulb fibre and water this to moisten.

Position: Set the bulbs in the compost surface – about 5 cm (2 in) apart if you are growing several.

Water: Fill with more bulb fibre. The top of the bulb should just project above the compost surface. Water to moisten the upper layer of fibre.

Store: Put the container in a cool dark place, such as a pantry, for around eight weeks. (The bulbs should not need further watering during this period, but check them periodically to make sure the fibre does not dry out.)

Light: When the flower buds are visible and showing a touch of colour, bring the container out into full light (but out of direct sunlight).

Bulbs: After flowering, either discard the bulbs or plant them out in the garden.

Note: Forced hyacinths can also be grown in special glasses that hold a single bulb suspended over a reservoir of water. Start them off in a cool room and out of bright sunlight. Keep topping up the water so it just touches the base of the bulb. Move the bulbs into a warm brightly lit room when the buds start to show colour.

Indoor Daffodils

Indoor daffodils such as *Narcissus* 'Soleil d'Or' and 'Paperwhite' need more light and do not need to be kept in the dark initially. The clusters of sweetly scented flowers are carried on tall stems, so these should be staked to prevent them from falling over. When planting the bulbs, insert a thin cane about 30 cm (12 in) long next to each one. Attach the stems to the canes loosely with wire or twine as they grow.

Narcissus 'Paperwhite'

Conservatories and Sun Rooms

While the majority of houseplants are quite happy in an ordinary living room, you'll greatly extend the range you can grow if you have a conservatory or sun room. You can create quite a jungle for sitting in.

Aspect

Most conservatories and sun rooms are designed to maximize the amount of light and warmth available, so are usually made as an extension on the sunny side of the house. Since they have a glass roof, the light is less directional than in most rooms (where it enters only through windows at the side) – light is also available from above. In practice, this means that they can get very hot, especially in summer. If the temperature is too high for you to be comfortable, it may well not please the plants either.

Top Tip

In a conservatory that's heated in winter, you can keep plants such as pelargoniums and osteospermums growing and flowering throughout the year.

Basket Cases

If you have a large plant such as a rubber plant, you can hang small orchids and rainforest cacti from the upper branches in special slatted wooden baskets. The stems of these will trail downwards, presenting the flowers at eye level. This replicates the way they grow in the wild.

Room at the Top

The extra headroom allows you to grow plants that would be much too large for the living room. You can allow plants such as the Swiss cheese plant (*Monstera deliciosa*), bougainvillea, oleander (*Nerium oleander*), the rubber plant (*Ficus elastica*) and weeping fig (*Ficus benjamina*) to reach tree-like proportions, so they shade plants at their feet.

Ficus benjamin
(weeping fig)

Caring for Plants

Summer

✓ To prevent the temperature climbing too high, open the doors, windows and roof vents on hot days.

✓ If necessary, put some shading across the roof, especially if leaves are close to the glass.

✓ Hose down the floor in the morning and the evening – the evaporation will lower the air temperature.

Winter

✓ If you keep the room heated over winter, keep watering the plants so they never dry out.

✓ If the conservatory is unheated, move the plants away from the glass and protect them from the worst of the cold.

Key Houseplants

The following are some of the plants most commonly grown for indoor display. They are all widely available and most are very easy to grow, being tolerant of the low light levels that are general indoors. 'H' stands for height, 'S' stands for spread.

Anthurium andraeanum

These plants are grown for their brilliant red spathes from which protrude long spikes of tiny creamy yellow flowers.
H and S 30–60 cm (12–24 in)

Aspidistra elatior

Cast iron plant
Among the most tolerant of houseplants, these tough plants with large green leaves withstand almost any amount of neglect.
H and S 60 cm (24 in)

Begonia rex

Rex begonias have brilliantly marked leaves – varying in size depending on the variety – often with a metallic sheen. Inconspicuous flowers sometimes appear. H and S 60 cm (24 in)

Aspidistra elatior (cast-iron plant)

Chlorophytum

Spider plant
These familiar plants, usually with striped leaves, will grow in a variety of situations. They are excellent in hanging baskets.
H 20 cm (8 in) or more, S 30 cm (12 in) or more.

Cissus rhombifolia

The glossy green leaves of this climber are divided into three. Tendrils on the stems will cling on to the support.
H 2 m (6 ft), S 1 m (3 ft)

Spider plant

Codiaeum variegatum

Croton

These plants
are grown for their
brilliantly coloured,
leathery-textured
leaves.
H 90 cm (36 in),
S 60 cm (24 in)

Codiaeum variegatum
(croton)

Cyclamen persicum

Indoor cyclamen have white, pink, brilliant
red or purple flowers (some are scented), in
autumn and winter. The petals can have frilly
edges. Plants die back and are completely
dormant in summer.
H 20 cm (8 in), S 15 cm (6 in)

Dieffenbachia seguine 'Exotica'

The large leaves of this plant are generously
splashed and mottled with creamy white.
H 90 cm (36 in), S 40 cm (16 in)

Ficus benjamina

Weeping fig
These easily grown shrubs or small trees can
have plain green or variegated leaves.
H 1.5 m (5 ft) or more, S 1.2 m (4 ft) or more.

Ficus elastica

Rubber plant
This familiar plant has large leathery, glossy
green leaves. Variegated forms are slower
growing.
H 2 m (6 ft) or more, S 1 m (3 ft) or more.

Gardenia

Glossy green leaves set off the sweetly
scented white flowers that appear in summer
and autumn. This plant must be grown in
ericaceous compost.
H and S 45 cm (18 in)

Hoya carnosa

Wax plant
This vigorous climber has clusters of
sweetly scented flowers among its thick
leathery leaves.
H 1.1 m (4 ft), S 45 cm (18 in)

Hoya carnosa (wax plant)

Hyacinthus

Hyacinth

Forced bulbs can be grown easily indoors to flower in mid to late winter. Flower)colours include white, pink, blue, purple and orange. H 30 cm (12 in), S 10 cm (4 in)

Jasminum polyanthum

Jasmine

This climber produces masses of deliciously scented flowers from late winter to early spring. H 90 cm (36 in) or more, S 60 cm (24 in) or more.

Maranta leuconeura

Prayer plant

The paddle-shaped leaves have pronounced veins and are strikingly marked with contrasting colours. H 30 cm (12 in), S 30 cm (12 in)

Monstera deliciosa

Monstera deliciosa

A robust climber with impressive large leaves that develop holes then split at the edges. H 3 m (10 ft), S 1 m (3 ft)

Narcissus 'Paperwhite' and 'Soleil d'Or'

Indoor daffodils grown for their clusters of small but sweetly scented flowers in late winter. The stems need staking. H 45 cm (18 in), S 15 cm (6 in)

Nerium oleander

A common street tree in warm climates, this can be grown as a shrub indoors, with regular pruning. Flowers are white or pink. H 90 cm (36 in), S 60 cm (24 in)

Plumbago auriculata

This scrambling climber has clusters of sky blue flowers from summer to early winter. H 2 m (6 ft), S 2 m (6 ft)

Plumbago auriculata

Saintpaulia
African violet
Pretty little plants with clusters of white, pink, purple, magenta or violet flowers that can be produced throughout the year.
H 15 cm (6 in), S 20 cm (8 in)

Sansevieria trifasciata 'Laurentii'
Mother-in-law's tongue
The thick upright leaves are boldly margined with yellow and are banded with silver – the plant always makes a bold statement.
H 60 cm (24 in), S 30 cm (1 in)

Schefflera elegantissima
A dramatic plant with strikingly toothed leaf margins.
H 2 m (6 ft), S 1 m (3 ft)

Sinningia
Gloxinia
Rosettes of velvety leaves are the perfect foil for the showy, trumpet-like flowers in a range of colours.
H 30 cm (12 in), S 30 cm (12 in)

Stephanotis floribunda
Wax flower
Intoxicatingly scented white flowers appear from spring to autumn among this climber's leathery leaves.
H 90 cm (36 in) or more, S 60 cm (24 in) or more.

Streptocarpus
Cape primrose
Wiry stems that rise from clusters of wrinkled leaves carry funnel-shaped flowers in a range of colours.
H 25 cm (10 in), S 25 cm (10 in)

Tradescantia
These trailing plants, ideal for hanging baskets, have green or purple leaves that are boldly marked with creamy white or silver.
H 15 cm (6 in), S 20 cm (8 in)

Sinningia
(gloxinia)

Cacti and Succulents

It's easy to get hooked on these plants, with their striking shapes and exotic flowers. Many are small enough to make a display on a windowsill, while others need more space in a well–lit room or conservatory.

A Range of Shapes and Sizes

These plants intrigue because of their overall appearance – most can be reluctant to flower, and the flowers are usually not long-lived. Some, like *Euphorbia canariensis*, have tall upward-thrusting stems. Others, such as *Echinocactus*, make dumpy barrel-like spheres or ovoids.

They can be covered in spines, fine needles or sharp hooks – or may be smooth-skinned. The old-man cactus (*Cephalocereus senilis*) is wrapped in a fine coating of white hairs. The money plant (*Crassula ovata*) looks like a little tree with thick, shiny, coin-like leaves. Species of *Lithops* look like little stones. A few, however, such as the Christmas cactus (*Schlumbergera*), are grown mainly for their white, pink or red flowers, usually produced in abundance.

What's the Difference Between a Cactus and a Succulent?

It's not the spines that make a cactus a cactus. Some succulents have spines and some cacti are smooth. What distinguishes the cacti are areoles (they are like little cushions or bumps) on the stems. There may be spines, needles or long hairs around the areoles – but these can be absent.

Displaying Cacti and Succulents

Although these plants can be grown in single pots, they are also suitable for grouping together in large shallow troughs – like a mini desert garden. Space the plants well, so each can be appreciated as an individual. Top the compost with sand or fine grit. Rainforest cacti, with their pendulous stems, can be stood on high shelves and allowed to cascade down but are also suitable for indoor hanging baskets (*see* Rainforest cacti, page 228).

Queens of the Desert

Mainly, cacti and succulents are plants of the desert. They have fleshy, swollen leaves or stems that look quite unlike those of other plants. These enable them to store water during prolonged hot, dry periods. Spines and hairs enable them to grab whatever moisture is available in the form of overnight mists – and also deter passing rodents from biting a chunk out of them.

Light

Desert cacti needas much light as possible year-round. They thrive on a sunny windowsill or in a bright conservatory.

Watering and Feeding

Water regularly during spring and summer. They can be kept dry during winter, when they are dormant, but be prepared to give some water if they appear to wither slightly (indicating they have exhausted their own stored water). These plants need feeding just as much as other plants. Use a cactus fertilizer when the plants are in full growth during spring and summer.

Handling Spiny Plants

Potting on or repotting a spiky plant can be tricky. Although you can wear stout gloves, a better way to get a good grip is to wrap a strip of folded paper around the plant, then grasp both ends tightly. Use this handle to lift the plant from the container.

Rainforest Cacti

A few cacti actually originate in cool tropical forests, where they grow in trees. They are quite distinct from desert cacti, with flattened, segmented stems and a trailing habit.

Note: While they thrive in ordinary plant pots, rainforest cacti also lend themselves to growing in hanging baskets. The basket should be suspended over a hard floor that you can wipe down (or you could place a large tray under it), to prevent water forming a puddle as it drains through. Turn the basket every two weeks in spring and summer so the plant grows evenly.

Light

These cacti need less light than desert types, so should be shaded from direct sun in summer. Put them in a brighter position in winter.

Watering and Feeding

Water regularly in spring and summer. In winter – when some types will be flowering – water to prevent the compost from drying out completely. Feed the plants during spring and summer when they are growing strongly. Do not feed while the plants are in flower.

Go Nocturnal

Cactus flowers are generally short-lived and may be open for only a day – or even a few hours – before dropping from the plant. Some open only at night. If you want to enjoy these, you need to stay up with a flask of coffee (or other beverage) to enjoy the flowers.

Note: As an extra reward for your vigil, the flowers of many of these plants are deliciously scented.

Key Cacti and Succulents

There is more diversity in this group of plants than is commonly supposed. The cacti and succulents described on the next two pages make good houseplants and give some idea of the range of plants available. 'H' stands for height, 'S' stands for spread.

Cephalocereus senilis

Old man cactus

The single columnar stem is covered with long, greyish or white hairs (hence the common name). This cactus seldom flowers as a houseplant.

H 25 cm (10 in), S 10 cm (4 in)

Crassula ovata

Money plant

The swollen, rounded leaves of this shrubby succulent are sometimes edged with red. Established plants look like miniature trees.

H 45cm (18 in), S 30 cm (12 in)

Echinocactus grusonii

Crassula ovata (money plant)

Echinocactus grusonii

These slow-growing cacti are sometimes called 'barrel' cacti because of their squat, swollen, ribbed bodies. They are very spiny. Only mature specimens flower.

H and S 38cm (15in) (flowering size)

Euphorbia canariensis

An impressive succulent with strongly upright, swollen, spiny, angled stems. Mature specimens can be tree-like.

H and S 90 cm (3 ft)

Euphorbia milii (crown of thorns)

Schlumbergera

These are the most popular rainforest cacti, with segmented, swollen stems. They produce their usually red flowers in autumn to winter.
H and S 30 cm (12 in)

Euphorbia milii
Crown of thorns
This thorny succulent has branching stems that carry bright red (occasionally yellow or salmon pink) flowers intermittently throughout the year. It is an undemanding plant that is easy to grow.
H 45 cm (18 in), S 30 cm (12 in)

Lithops
Living stones
These very slow-growing succulents really do look like pebbles, so be sure to surround them with contrasting stone chippings. Most have a pair of very thick leaves that are fused at the base. Large flowers appear between the leaves.
H and S 2.5 cm (1 in), more or less.

Schlumbergera

Orchids and Their Care

With their glamorous flowers, orchids have become increasingly popular as houseplants. They flower reliably for weeks on end (sometimes months) and, contrary to popular belief, many are surprisingly easy to grow.

Phalaenopsis

Easy Orchids

Phalaenopsis – or moth orchids, so-called because of the shape of the flowers – are the easiest of all to grow. These orchids have been specially bred to thrive in centrally heated sitting rooms and can be guaranteed to flower for a long period. Besides these, cymbidiums, dendrobiums and oncidiums make excellent houseplants.

Did You Know?

In the wild, most orchids are epiphytes – they grow in trees, usually in tropical and subtropical rainforest, rather than being rooted in the ground like other plants.

Phalaenopsis

Phalaenopsis have tall, arching stems with clusters of flowers at their tips. Once the whole cluster has faded, cut the stem back to a node lower down. (The nodes look like tiny leaves scattered down the stem. Make the cut just above one near the top.) A new flowering stem will soon appear. Once these flowers have finished, cut back the stems to the base and give the plant a rest for up to six weeks.

Cymbidiums

Cymbidiums are as easy to grow as phalaenopsis –
though they prefer a cooler room – but can be much
more reluctant to flower. A period of fluctuating
temperatures seems to stimulate flower production.
The simplest way to achieve this is to place the plants
outdoors from mid summer to early autumn, in a
sheltered, shaded position. The drop in temperature at
night provides the necessary stimulus. Bring the plants
back indoors before the first frosts are expected. Flower
spikes will appear in late winter.

Cymbidium

Resting Orchids

Orchids are like actors – though many can be
productive year-round, they are best if given a rest
period occasionally, usually in winter. Put the plants
in a brightly lit place, reduce watering and stop
feeding. Return the plants to a more shaded
position as the days start to lengthen in spring, then
start watering and feeding again.

Caring for Orchids

Many people are put off keeping orchids at home because they consider them to be a specialist
plant that needs a lot of care and attention. However, if you meet their few simple requirements,
such as correct light levels and type of compost, orchids will reward you with a flourish of
stunning, often long-lasting, colour.

Composts

Orchids need special composts that are usually coarse and fibrous allowing for swift drainage. The purpose of the compost is to stabilize the roots rather than to deliver nutrients to the plant. In the wild, orchids get what they need from minerals dissolved in rainwater that washes down over the plants (*see also* Feeding, below).

Light

Orchids need good light to grow well but do not tolerate bright sun for long periods. A light position in a well-lit room is fine, or on a windowsill that's shaded from direct sun. In the winter, when orchids are mainly resting, they should be allowed as much light as possible, so moving them next to a sunny window is fine. On cold nights, move them away from the glass before bedtime, or the sudden drop in temperature may damage the plant.

Watering

Water orchids freely when they are in full growth – usually in spring and summer. Water from a can, directly into the compost, not from above – water may settle among the leaves, leading to rotting. During winter, water more sparingly, just enough to keep the compost from drying out fully.

Feeding

Orchids have a low nutrient requirement. Either use a dedicated orchid fertilizer, either watered over the roots or (better) sprayed over the leaves, or apply a tomato fertilizer at a quarter strength.

Misting

Bearing in mind that orchids are rainforest plants, most appreciate a certain level of humidity. A centrally heated room may be too warm for most – apart from phalaenopsis. Lightly mist over the plants twice a day with a spray turned to its finest setting. The main purpose of misting, however, is to lower the temperature around the plants. If you keep your orchids in a cooler room – for instance, a dining room that is used only periodically – misting is unnecessary.

Staking

The flowers of orchids are usually so large – or there are so many of them – that the stems have to be staked to stop them keeling over. If a new flower stem appears on an orchid, insert a thin cane into the compost next to it (taking care not to damage the roots). As it grows, attach the stem to the cane with special plastic clips or twists of wire or string.

Key Orchids

Most of the orchids that are sold today are hybrids that are easy to maintain and bring into flower. Some of the most popular types are described below. Rarer orchids are available from specialist nurseries.

Cymbidium

Depending on their size, these orchids are classified as standard, intermediate or miniature. At up to 1 m (3ft) tall, standards are too large for most interiors. Cymbidiums appreciate a firm compost (rockwool is ideal) and flower best when pot-bound.

H 45 cm (18 in), S 30 cm (12 in) (intermediate; miniatures are smaller)

Miltoniopsis

Dendrobium

Dendrobiums have bamboo-like stems and flamboyant flowers, similar to cymbidiums. Hybrids (such as 'Prima Donna') are easy to grow. Plants can be placed outdoors (in a sheltered spot) in summer.

Miltoniopsis

These are sometimes referred to as pansy orchids, owing to the distinctive markings on the flowers (which open flat and may be scented). These orchids can be in flower virtually throughout the year, but are best if rested in winter.

Odontoglossum

These orchids show more variety than others. Some odontoglossums have large flowers, others have much smaller ones that are carried in abundance on branching stems. The majority flower in a nine-monthly cycle, which means they flower at different times each year.

Phalaenopsis

Moth orchids

Phalaenopsis are the most popular of all the orchids, with beautiful white, pink, purple, yellow, red or orange flowers. They are capable of flowering throughout the year, but benefit from a winter rest.

Odontoglossum

Hydroponics

Hydroponics – or, more properly, hydroculture – is a means of growing plants in water. This very clean method – no compost is involved – is commonly used for large plant displays in office foyers and public interior spaces.

Growing Media

Instead of traditional composts, plants are held in special inert media that merely support the roots. Suitable materials include:

- Clay pebbles
- Perlite
- Vermiculite
- Rockwool

Clay pebbles are the most widely used. They are clean, pH neutral, pH stable and well suited to most systems. Perlite and vermiculite are sometimes used together – perlite is airy and drains well, while vermiculite holds on to some moisture. Rockwool is both air- and water-retentive.

Dieffenbachia

Systems

A number of hydroponics systems are available. Very expensive models incorporate pumps for the water supply and even lights, allowing you to manipulate growth rates – for instance, for accelerating the development of seedlings in winter. Simpler systems comprise a special pot with a recess at the base (to hold a fertilizer cartridge) that sits in an outer decorative container (any container can be used, but it must be watertight). Water is poured into the gap between the containers to form a shallow reservoir at the base. The growing medium absorbs the water – which is then available to the plants – through capillary action. A special gauge that sits in the growing medium indicates the amount of water in the reservoir. Top it up when this gives a minimum reading.

Note: Although the reservoir always contains water, it is never so deep that plant roots actually sit in it.

Preparing Plants

Plants for hydroponics are available from specialist nurseries. They have usually been raised from cuttings and have spent their whole life grown this way. You can use plants you already own, however, as follows:

 Remove the plant from its pot and soak the rootball in water for up to an hour.
 Gently tease out the compost from among the roots with your fingers.
Carefully wash the roots under running water to eliminate all traces of compost.

Note: Plants grown hydroponically develop 'water roots', which are much more brittle than ordinary roots. It can be difficult to transplant a hydroponically grown plant into conventional compost.

Anthurium

Plants for hydroculture

Besides many bulbs, cacti and orchids, the following plants are suitable.

Anthurium	Euphorbia milii (crown of thorns)
Cissus	Ficus benjamina (weeping fig)
Codiaeum	Saintpaulia (African violet)
Dieffenbachia	Schefflera

Caring for Plants Indoors

Since they are growing in an artificial environment, plants indoors need more attention than their counterparts outdoors, which are kept fresh by regular rainfall. The following details their (modest) requirements.

Composts

Standard potting composts (*see* p.xxx) are suitable for most houseplants, though cacti and succulents (*see* pages 226–31) and orchids (pages 232–36) need specific mixes.

Pot on or repot houseplants in spring, if they have outgrown their containers. The procedure is the same as for outdoor container plants (*see* page 68).

Light

Most houseplants need good light, but most do not like direct sunlight, particularly around midday. If they are on a windowsill, put up some form of shading in summer to protect the leaves from scorching – glass will magnify the strength of the sun's rays – or move them into the room well away from burning rays. If plants are near a window, make sure the leaves do not touch the glass. Beads of moisture may collect there that can lead to rotting.

Temperature

An even temperature suits the majority of houseplants. Most will not tolerate freezing temperatures, and certainly not for prolonged periods. Steeply fluctuating temperatures can also cause problems – an ambient temperature is best. Kitchens and bathrooms, which can at times be hot and steamy then cold at others, are much less suitable than sitting rooms that are predominantly warm, or spare bedrooms that are generally cool.

If you grow your plants on a windowsill, move them away from the glass on cold winter nights – the temperature may drop too low for comfort. They can stay where they are if there is a thick curtain between them and the glass that can be drawn at night. Few houseplants like being in a draught. A position near a door or window that is regularly opened is best avoided.

Stay Cool

Centrally heated sitting rooms can actually be too hot for some houseplants. The easiest way to lower the temperature is to raise the humidity around them. You can either mist over the plants (using a spray turned to its finest setting) or – simpler – stand the pots on trays filled with special clay pellets. Fill the tray with water. The pellets absorb the water, then release it gradually. Alternatively, place shallow saucers of water among the plants. This will raise the humidity level as the water evaporates.

Watering

Tap water – straight from the cold water supply – is fine for nearly all plants. Water from a watering can, directly over the roots, to avoid splashing the leaves. If the water is hard, you may see a white residue appearing on the compost surface and the outsides of the pot. Boiling the water first, then allowing it to cool, will prevent this happening. In winter, allow the water to stand for half an hour or so after drawing it, so it is closer to room temperature when you deliver it to the plants. This will avoid shocking the roots.

Feeding

Houseplants need feeding just as much as outdoor plants. It's easiest to use a dedicated houseplant fertilizer, formulated either for foliage plants or flowering plants (alternatively, use a seaweed extract for leaves and a tomato feed for flowers). Feed the plants every week or every two weeks when they are growing strongly, in spring to mid summer. A common mistake is to overfeed – which can be counterproductive. Excess fertilizer can be toxic to plants and result in soft growth that is very disease-prone.

Summer Holidays

Houseplants like being in the fresh air as much as we do. During the mild weather of summer, they can spend time outdoors. Choose a place out of direct sunlight, which can scorch delicate leaves. The plants will still need regular watering, so a spot near the house, with its water supply, is best. Bring the plants back indoors at the end of summer (apart from cymbidiums: see page 233) and before the nights get significantly colder.

Caring for Houseplants When Away

If you are planning to be away from home for a period, you may be concerned that your precious plants will dry out. A number of strategies can keep them happy, as follows:

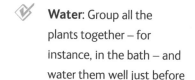 **Water**: Group all the plants together – for instance, in the bath – and water them well just before leaving.

Matting: Stand the containers on a length of capillary matting. Place one end of the matting in a bowl or trough of water. (The matting will draw up the water gradually.)

Wicks: Place a bowl of water among the plants. Trail the ends of absorbent wicks in the water, then bury the free ends in the compost of each plant.

 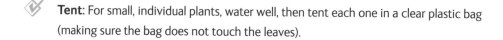

Top Tip

Houseplants can also be used in your summer containers, window boxes and hanging baskets.

Tent: For small, individual plants, water well, then tent each one in a clear plastic bag (making sure the bag does not touch the leaves).

A Cast-iron Constitution

Aspidistra elatior often goes by the common name of cast-iron plant – because it is so tolerant of poor growing conditions and virtually impossible to kill. There is a very attractive variegated form, 'Variegata', with boldly striped leaves.

Because They're Worth it

Various leaf shine products will help keep leaves free of dust and other marks (possibly made as a result of misting or splashes when watering). Not only do these improve the appearance of the plant, but they will help keep it disease-free. Wipe the leaves in early spring to freshen up a plant after its winter rest, then throughout spring and summer to keep them looking good.

Top Tip

To revive neglected plants, stand them in the shower tray, then turn the shower on (cold setting). Leave the plants for 20 minutes or so. Allow the pots to drain before returning them to their normal positions.

Grooming Houseplants

Plants indoors do not need pruning in the same way as plants outdoors. But to keep them healthy and looking good, snip off all dead leaves, stems and flowers as soon as you see them. Use either florists' scissors or household scissors (provided they are sharp and pointed). You can also do an effective job with finger and thumb, provided you are reasonably dextrous.

Pests and Diseases

Indoor plants are prone to a number of pests and diseases that normally do not cause problems outdoors. In the closed environment of the house, pests can multiply rapidly, and there are no natural predators to keep their numbers down. Diseases can rapidly spread from plant to plant, especially in displays where leaves touch.

Preventing Problems

Plants that are under stress are more likely to fall victim to pests and diseases. Doing the following will help keep them at bay:

- ✔ **Water:** Keep plants well watered when they are growing strongly, without letting them sit in water.

- ✔ **Feed:** Feed plants with a suitable fertilizer as necessary.

- ✔ **Prune:** Cut off faded flowers and all dead material from plants.

- ✔ **Move:** Turn plants regularly to keep them growing evenly.

Separate sick plants from healthy ones

> **Separate**: Make sure plants are not crowded too closely together for long periods, which can cause stagnant air (in which fungi can breed) around them.

> **Isolate**: If you do have a sick plant, move it well away from other plants while you treat it, to prevent the pest or disease from moving to the healthy ones.

Pests

Pests that affect houseplants are mainly invertebrates – insects, mites and other tiny creatures. Most are easy to control, provided you take prompt action before they have a chance to breed and proliferate.

Aphids

Sometimes also called greenfly (though they can also be black, grey or orange), these tiny insects suck sap from young, soft stems and leaves and deposit honeydew.

Control: Spray with a pesticide as soon as you see the pests, or dislodge them with a strong jet of water (best done outdoors).

Ants

Ants do not in themselves cause much damage, but they are attracted to the honeydew that certain pests excrete. As they go about collecting this sweet, sticky substance, they will also pick up the pests' eggs and transfer them to the next plant they visit. If you have to deal with any honeydew-secreting pest, also put down some ant killer to prevent spread of the pest.

Mealybugs

Small pests with a fluffy white coating, which cluster on stems and the undersides of leaves. The plants wilt and shed their leaves.

Control: Wipe off the pest with a damp cloth, then spray with an insecticide.

Red Spider Mite

The sap-sucking mites are microscopic – what you'll see is a telltale webbing between leaves and stems. The plant is weakened and leaves are shed prematurely.

Control: This creature multiplies fast in hot, dry conditions, so keep plants cool by misting and watering regularly. Treat with a pesticide as soon as you notice any webbing.

Scale Insects

These tiny creatures are protected by hard brown shells and cluster on the undersides of leaves, feeding on sap and dropping honeydew on to the leaves below. The casing makes them resistant to most pesticides.

Control: Wipe the scales off with a damp cloth (scrub firmer leaves with an old toothbrush), then spray the plant with a pesticide to prevent further infestations.

Scale insects

Vine Weevil

The adult weevils eat holes in the edges of leaves, but more damage is done by the grubs. These hatch in summer from eggs laid on the compost surface, then tunnel into the compost to feed on plant roots (and the tubers of cyclamen and begonias).

Control: If you spot the adults in summer, treat the plant with an insecticide applied as a root drench (to kill the grubs). Alternatively, kill the grubs with a parasitic nematode (available by mail order).

Whitefly

These tiny moth-like insects produce green youngsters that feed on sap and deposit honeydew. Leaves turn yellow and are shed by the plant. Whiteflies can breed rapidly.

Control: Spray at the first sign of attack and repeat regularly to prevent numbers building up.

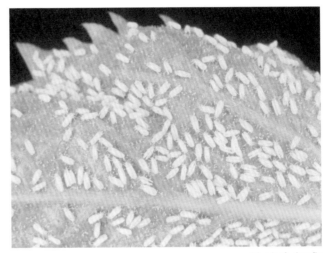

Silverleaf whitefly

Diseases

Plant diseases are caused mainly by fungi and bacteria. They often affect plants that are not growing strongly. Keeping plants correctly watered and fed (without overfeeding) is the best way to keep them healthy.

Botrytis/Grey Mould

This fluffy grey mould appears on the leaves of many plants, often proliferating during damp weather.

Control: Cut off and destroy affected parts. Check whether mould is also growing on the compost surface – repot in fresh compost if so. Spray affected plants with a fungicide, then reduce watering and misting and improve ventilation.

Powdery mildew

Powdery Mildew

White patches of fungus appear on the upper surfaces of leaves. This can spread to stems and flowers.

Control: Cut off and destroy affected parts of the plant, then spray with a fungicide. Avoid overcrowding the plants.

Rusts

Brown spots appear on the undersides of leaves – often on pelargoniums.

Control: Cut off and burn affected leaves. Spray affected plants with a fungicide and improve ventilation around them.

Sooty Mould

This black fungus grows on the upper surfaces of leaves, on honeydew deposited by a number of pests. The mould is unsightly and leads to poor growth.

Control: Wipe off the mould with a damp cloth, then identify and treat the pest that has dropped the honeydew.

Viruses

Several plants are prone to particular viruses, which cause stunted growth and/or yellow spots and patches on leaves. Viruses are sometimes present in plants when you buy them, or are introduced by insect pests via cuts and tears in the plant's tissues. Viruses cannot be treated. If you have a plant affected by a virus, it should be destroyed.

checklist

✓ **Positioning:** Find the best position for houseplants. Some may need a lot of room or have limited tolerance of low light levels. None like being in a draught.

✓ **Bulbs:** Plant forced bulbs in autumn for mid winter flowering.

✓ **Cacti and succulents:** Make mini desert gardens in shallow pans and troughs, planted with desert cacti and succulents. Keep them in a sunny, warm position. Rainforest cacti are tolerant of lower light levels and temperatures.

✓ **Water sparingly:** Keep desert plants dry over winter (unless they start to shrivel). Water rainforest types just enough to keep the compost moist.

✓ **Orchids:** Grow orchids in a room where the temperature does not fluctuate too widely. *Phalaenopsis* are ideally suited to centrally heated living rooms. Water and feed orchids when they are in full growth.

✓ **Cymbidium orchids:** To encourage cymbidiums to flower, place them outdoors from mid to late summer.

✓ **Support orchids:** Support the tall flowering stems of orchids with thin stakes to prevent the weight of the flowers from bending and breaking them.

✓ **Rest orchids:** Rest orchids over winter. Reduce watering and move them into as light a position as possible during the darker months.

Calendar of Care

The following calendar provides a quick reference to what you can be doing throughout the year to maintain long-term plantings and plan for seasonal displays.

Early Spring

- [ ] Dead-head bulbs that have finished flowering. If you intend to keep the bulbs for next year, feed them and then allow them to die back naturally.
- [ ] Most plants are coming into vigorous growth. Begin watering and feeding them regularly.
- [ ] Protect the new foliage of plants from slugs.
- [ ] Remove any dead leaves and stems from grasses to make way for new growth.
- [ ] Hand-pollinate peach trees when in flower.

Mid Spring

- [ ] Buy and plant lily bulbs, dahlias and tuberous begonias from garden centres (unless you have previously ordered these from bulb merchants).
- [ ] Give topiary specimens their first clip of the year.
- [ ] Shear over roses in containers.
- [ ] Pot on or repot any plants that have outgrown their allotted container.
- [ ] Top-dress any that are too large to handle easily.
- [ ] Sow seed of outdoor tomatoes and other annual plants for use outdoors in summer.

Late Spring

- [ ] Buy bedding plants for summer containers from a garden centre, unless you have raised your own plants from seed.
- [ ] Plant hanging baskets, large containers and window boxes for summer display, using bedding plants, fuchsias, pelargoniums and tender perennials.
- [ ] In frost-prone areas, protect plants from the worst of the weather until all danger of frost has passed.
- [ ] Pinch-prune fuchsias to encourage bushiness.
- [ ] Decorate or customize containers ready for summer displays.

Early Summer

- [ ] In frost-prone areas, it's now usually safe to put out hanging baskets, window boxes and other containers planted with tender plants for summer display.
- [ ] Water plants frequently, especially on dry days, and keep feeding them.

Mid Summer

- ☐ Water plants frequently during what is usually the hottest part of the year.
- ☐ During very hot periods – or if you are planning to go away – move all the plants together into a shady spot so that they will dry out less quickly.
- ☐ Carry on clipping topiary plants to keep them looking neat.
- ☐ Keep dead-heading flowering annuals and tender perennials to keep them producing fresh flowers.
- ☐ Dead-head roses.
- ☐ Harvest tomatoes as they ripen.
- ☐ Harvest strawberries from strawberry plants.
- ☐ On indoor plants, watch out for signs of pests and diseases, which often proliferate during warm weather. Turn plants regularly so that they grow evenly.

Late Summer

- ☐ Order bulbs for next spring's containers.
- ☐ To overwinter fuchsias, stand them in a sunny, warm position to ripen the wood.
- ☐ Give topiary plants their last clip of the year.
- ☐ Continue harvesting tomatoes.

Autumn

- ☐ Empty out containers used for summer bedding plants. Wash out the containers and then store them for use next year.
- ☐ Empty pots containing dahlias, tuberous begonias and cannas. Dry off the bulbs. Store them in a cool, dry place for use next year.
- ☐ Buy spring bulbs (unless already ordered). Plant them up for next year's display.
- ☐ Take cuttings of tender perennials for overwintering indoors.
- ☐ Keep watering camellias in containers to make sure they build their flower buds for next year.
- ☐ Sow sweet pea seeds in a sheltered place outdoors.
- ☐ Reduce watering for houseplants and stop feeding them altogether. Plant up forced bulbs for winter display.

Winter

- ☐ Buy small hellebores, cyclamen, heathers and winter pansies in flower for use in containers and window boxes, along with dwarf shrubs and conifers.
- ☐ If frost is forecast, provide suitable protection for plants overnight. Move them into a sheltered area or wrap up the container to prevent the roots from freezing.
- ☐ Prune fig trees while they are dormant.
- ☐ Give most houseplants, especially orchids, maximum light by positioning them near sunny windows. On cold nights, move them well away from the glass to avoid freezing.
- ☐ Bring forced hyacinths kept in the dark into daylight.

Further Reading

Allen Smith, P., *P. Allen Smith's Container Gardens: 60 Container Recipes to Accent Your Garden*, Clarkson Potter, 2005

Baldwin, D. L., *Succulent Container Gardens: Design Eye-Catching Displays with 350 Easy-Care Plants*, Timber Press, 2010

Brickell, C., *The Encyclopedia of Plants and Flowers*, Dorling Kindersley, 2010

Greenwood, P., *The Ultimate Book of Gardening Hints & Tips*, Dorling Kindersley, 2009

Hamilton, O., *Hip Houseplants*, DK Adult, 2001

Harrison, J., *Vegetable, Fruit and Herb Growing in Small Spaces*, Right Way, 2010

Hessayon, D. G., *The House Plant Expert*, Pan Britannica, 1992

Hessayon, D. G., *The Pest and Weed Expert*, Expert, 2007

McHoy, P., *The Complete Houseplant Book: The Essential Guide to Successful Indoor Gardening*, Lorenz Books, 1998

Mikolajski, A., *1001 Garden Questions Answered: Expert Solutions to Everyday Gardening Dilemmas*, Lorenz Books, 2010

Mikolajski, A., *Hanging Baskets: Create Stunning Seasonal Displays for Your Garden*, Anness, 2002

Nichols McGee, R. M. and Stuckey, M., *McGee & Stuckey's Bountiful Container: Create Container Gardens of Vegetables, Herbs, Fruits, and Edible Flowers*, Workman Publishing Company, 2002

Nilsson, M. and Arvidsson, C., *Concrete Garden Projects: Easy & Inexpensive Containers, Furniture, Water Features & More*, Timber Press, 2011

Peacock, P., *Patio Produce: How to Cultivate a Lot of Home-grown Vegetables from the Smallest Possible Space*, Spring Hill, 2009

Rodale, R., *The Basic Book of Organic Gardening*, Ballantine Books, Inc, 1993

Rogers, R., *Pots in the Garden: Expert Design & Planting Techniques*, Timber Press, 2007

Spence, I., *RHS Gardening Through The Year: Your Month-By-Month Guide to what to do when in the Garden*, Dorling Kindersley, 2009

Strauss, R., *Crops in Pots: Growing Vegetables, Fruits & Herbs in Pots, Containers & Baskets*, Flame Tree Publishing, 2011

Titchmarsh, A., *How to Be a Gardener: Back to Basics*, BBC Books, 2002

Thomas, C., *Gardeners' World - 101 Ideas for Pots: Foolproof Recipes for Year-round Colour*, BBC Books, 2007

Websites

www.allgardenpots.com/
A website dedicated to all things concerning 'practical container gardening'. There are even DIY projects that do interesting things with pots to make your garden even more beautiful.

www.bbc.co.uk/digin
The BBC's online campaign encourages domestic vegetable cultivation and cooking in a fun, accessible manner.

www.bbc.co.uk/gardening/basics/techniques/
The BBC's gardening homepage provides basic growing techniques for the budding gardener.

www.bhg.com
Better Homes and Gardens magazine's online resource has festive ideas, special tips and design plans for the perfect home garden.

www.burgonandball.com
Website of the manufacturing tool specialists Burgon & Ball. Visit this site to shop for high-quality gardening utensils.

www.container-gardens.com
A small site dedicated to everything for container gardening.

www.davesgarden.com
Claiming to be the 'hands down favourite website of gardeners around the world', this site offers gardening advice from members' forums and a useful list of approved gardening product companies and websites.

www.deroma.com
A site dedicated to selling Deroma terracotta products. Their pots range from classic to innovative, and are perfect for container gardening.

www.finegardening.com
A great source of information for container gardening how-to and design, as well as articles and tips on all different gardening styles.

www.gardenguides.com
An extensive resource with linked articles about design, pests, gardening phases, plants and more.

www.gardenweb.com
Hosts a number of logs and forums, as well as articles on gardening and an 'Ask the Experts' section.

www.haxnicks.co.uk
The website for Haxnicks gardening company. You can buy their innovative products online and get helpful advice on growing all sorts of plants by reading their blog.

www.organicgardeningguru.com/
A comprehensive resource for gardeners interested in growing organically. Learn tips and tricks, terminology and how to go green with a green thumb.

www.unwins.co.uk
Unwins is a valuable supplier of vegetable seeds, all carefully selected and picked by hand.

www.urban-allotments.com/
A city-based website dedicated to growing food in small-space gardens. They have everything you need to get a garden started.

Index